I Am God

Seven Magickal Steps to Personal Divinity

I Am God

Seven Magickal Steps to Personal Divinity

By Lilith

© Copyright 2013

Copyright © 2013 by Lilith of the Wildwood
ISBN 978-1-291-27572-8

All rights reserved. No part of this publication may be reproduced or transmitted in any form or by any means without the prior written consent of the author and copyright owner.

To Jenna,
my beautiful and
inspirational daughter.
You are forever my teacher.

A Note:

The views expressed in this book are my personal opinion and my understanding of the universe, the now, and the long forgotten past. I believe that all history is conjecture as we can only make educated guesses at the meaning of the clues that have been left behind. As a mystic, I also believe that perception of current events is based purely on one's own personal perspective. The 'history' and all the other writing in this book is a truth that I see. It is therefore my personal 'her-story'. I will not attempt to prove or justify my ideas as fact, as they are based on my reality, my experience, my understanding through personal research, and my explorations and communications during my magickal journeys.

Table of Contents

Introduction	**1**
About the Author	**5**
Roots	**7**
Mysticism	7
Religion	7
Step onto Your Own Path	11
Magick	13
A New Story	**14**
Lilith Rising	**17**
The Old Stories	**31**
Original Sin	31
The Myth of Woman as Demon	33
The Culture of Control	35
A Disempowering Leadership	36
Secrets	37
Steps to Change	**39**
Illuminate Yourself	39
Are you Ready to Bite the Apple?	40
How to Use this Book	41
Journal – Your Personal Sacred Text	42
Experiences of Be-coming	42
Lilith Speaks	**45**
1 – Step into Awareness	**47**
Meditation – The Core Practice	**49**
What is Meditation?	50
Transformation and Healing	51
Expanded Consciousness	59
Intuition	59
Psychic Ability	60
Breath – Beginning and End	**61**
Foundation Breath meditation	63

Body – the Manifest Being	**66**
Body Sensation Meditation	68
Thought – the Stream of Delusion	**70**
Thought Awareness Meditation	72
2 – Step into Being	**75**
Senses	**77**
Day 1: Sensation	78
Day 2: Hearing	81
Day 3: Smell	84
Day 4: Taste	86
Day 5: Sight	88
Day 6: The Sixth Sense	90
Environment	**92**
Walking Meditation	93
Eating Meditation	95
Outer World Meditation	97
Other People	**99**
Re-action in Conversation	101
Re-action in Conflict	103
Re-action during Sexual Connection	105
3 – Step into Responsibility	**109**
Release Fear from the Mind	**111**
Clear old belief patterns	114
A New Internal Story – Angelic Love	116
Release Fear from the Body	**118**
Facial Tension Meditation	120
Body Tension Meditation	122
Offer your Body New Possibilities	**124**
Smile Meditation	125
Postures Meditation	126
Authentic Movement Meditation	129

4 – Step into Expanded Consciousness — 133
I Am Vibration — 135
- The Four (5) Elements — 136
- Earth — 139
- Water — 141
- Fire — 143
- Air — 145
- Spirit — 147

Understanding Ritual — 148
- Ritual of the Sacred Circle – The Function — 150

5 – Step into Power — 163
Awakening to Ritual — 165
- Clothing — 166
- Cleansing — 166
- Establish Thought-Forms — 167
- Make the Ritual your Own — 170

The Ritual of the Sacred Circle — 173
- Call the Spirit of Air — 173
- Call the Spirit of Fire — 175
- Call the Spirit of Water — 177
- Call the Spirit of Earth — 179
- Call the Centre — 181
- Call the Higher Power – Spirit — 183
- Release the circle — 184

Explore the Astral World — 185
- Astral Travel – Journey to Other Realms — 186
- Astral Journeys to the Vibrational Elements — 188
- To Begin Every Journey — 190
- To End Every Journey — 191
- Journey to Earth — 192
- Journey to Water — 194
- Journey to Fire — 196

Journey to Air	198
Journey to Spirit	200
6 – Step into the Boundless	**203**
Cosmic Magick – As Above, So Below	**205**
Day and Night	**207**
The Moon	207
Moon Bathing	208
Celebrate the Moon	209
Prayers to the Moon	210
Astral Journey to the Moon	211
The Sun	213
Sun Bathing	213
Prayers to the Sun	214
Astral Journey to the Sun	216
Awakening to Seasonal Shifts	**218**
The Wheel of the Year	**219**
Align with Winter Solstice – Awaken	221
Align with Imbolc – Inspire	223
Align with Spring Equinox – Nurture	225
Align with Beltane – Create	227
Align with Summer Solstice – Thrive	229
Align with Lammas – Produce	231
Align with Autumn Equinox – Gather	233
Align with Samhain – Release	235
Planetary Power	**237**
7 Planetary Rituals	238
Mercury	240
Venus	241
Mars	242
Jupiter	243
Saturn	244
Uranus	245

Neptune	246
Pluto	247
Travel to the Outer Cosmos	248

7 – Step into Unity — 249
Become the Divine Creator — 251
Magickal Manifestation	252
The Use and Abuse of Magick	254
Magickal Tools	256
Magickal Methods	257
Magickal Manifestation Ritual	258

Meet your Divine Self — 265
Child	267
Adult	269
Elder	272
The Divine Marriage	275
Divine Union – Sacred Sex Magick	279

Know Everything, Be Everywhere — 285
Cellular and Energetic Healing	285
Heal Traumatic Memories	288
Inter-dimensional Travel	290
Speak Your Divine Truth	293

Know Unity — 295
Unity Breath Meditation	297

Here's where I'll Leave You to Explore...	**301**
Lilith Speaks	**303**
Appendix 1 – Before All Magickal Work	305
Appendix 2 – After All Magickal Work	316
Appendix 3 – Condensed Ritual of the Sacred Circle	318

Introduction

This book, and all pure mystical practice, begins with the premise that you are perfect. You are a reflection of the infinite vibration of All, and you are therefore Divine. However, in monotheist world religions, such as Judaism, Islam, and Christianity, their words for 'God' describe a male, one-and-only, supreme, all knowing, and powerful creator of the universe that is well beyond your reach. It may or may not come as a surprise that this, of course, is a myth – a fairy tale that has been perpetuated in order to generate fear and control within cultures and to keep you from the knowledge of your own divine wisdom. If there is a great all-seeing 'Father' then who are we but perpetual children? Due to the fear of his punishment, these 'children' believe that they have no choices, no rights, no power, and no control.

The 'God' myth is a bastardisation of the preceding ancient wisdom that ALL is ONE. According to this wisdom, there IS a supreme, all knowing, and powerful creator, but it is not a bearded man in the sky, it is YOU – you and everything in the universe bundled together in one infinite ALL. The religious myths have been created in order to keep this knowledge from you – how could the religious leaders even attempt to control us if we were aware of our own immense power? By separating us from the ecstasy, the bliss, and the infinite love that comes from the experience of embodying this Unity, these myths keep people lonely and scared.

People desperately search for connection. They look to friends, family, lovers, and religions for love and acceptance. They may find it there – the shared experiences and shared devotion, and the apparent enduring and eternal love of God, can feel extremely fulfilling. But people, and these religions, tend to be judgemental and fear driven. Their love and approval depends on you behaving according to their expectations and rules. If you break the rules you will feel the limited and conditional nature of this 'love' and you may experience it being taken away. This, together with the threat of the wrath of God, is the perfect deterrent to rule breaking. It ultimately leads to the painful choice between a life of pretence or the experience of rejection – both of which can only create more loneliness.

For human animals exile is one of the biggest fears and, from a very early age, they tend to choose pretence over rejection. They find themselves living in a constant, although often unconscious, onslaught of anxiety-raising thoughts and fears about what others think. They prefer to follow rules, to say 'yes' when they mean 'no', and they attempt to please people and authority figures in order to appear acceptable, and therefore to be loved. This creates pain and the limitation of expression in everything, including: work, play, creativity, speech, clothing, physical appearance, sexuality, gender, and relationships. This leads to emotional and physical imbalances and a shrinking of the spirit.

I believe we all have the capacity for enlightenment, bliss, and fearless expression, and we all have the right to follow our chosen path to happiness and fulfilment, but none of this can be found if you are bound by fears of disapproval.

In order to clear these fears, and to learn to live in freedom without the need for approval, healing is necessary. But many people even fear the healing process itself. This is not surprising as it is often imagined as being a process of pain and suffering. With many of the current healing methods it often is – some are brutal, and many even create more trauma. However, it is possible to heal through joy and pleasure just as much as, if not more than, through anguish and pain. Through pleasure, and feelings of internal love and comfort, you can re-write your traumatic memories. The experience of real ecstasy during healing can help to re-frame your thinking and to release these fears. But pleasure and ecstasy have been given a bad name by these religions, and people often feel uncomfortable about experiencing or expressing these feelings. However, ecstasy can lead us to the most profound healing, and it is our divine right to feel it.

It can be felt in the experience of Oneness – realisation of Unity is blissful. When you know you are One with All you are never alone, you no longer need the approval of other people or an external God, and therefore you are free. With this freedom comes an awakening of the deeper consciousness and a capacity to truly love. When you BE love your touch, your word, your energy field, and everything you do becomes a flow of healing for yourself and others and you will finally discover the connection you have been searching for.

I want to help you find it.

Having cleared away the false myths, the unnecessary dogma, and the fear based superstition of religion and ritual, I have revealed a simple, yet powerful and beautiful, mystical practice that can be followed alone or with a group. It will enable you to step away from the deep-set fears that were created from your childhood experience and from the influence of a monotheist culture.

This book takes you on a journey from your inner world to the outer cosmos. It offers a simple yet powerful practice for personal and ecstatic discovery. Using story, magick, ritual, sacred sex, breath, meditation, self-exploration, and the ecstatic state, it leads you on a path of false-self destruction. When there is no fear you are left with only authentic truth, free expression, expansive love, and absolute presence. You are left with the God that is YOU.

About the Author

I am a mystic. I search for truth by looking within and by exploring the universe I experience around me. This book is a collection of some of the foundation rituals and practices that I have developed, and that have supported my personal transformations and those of my students, over my many years of magickal experience.

Welcome to my world. My first memory is one of entering the vibrational level of reality. I experienced my edges spreading out around me until I joined with the molecular structure of the furniture in the room. The edges of the molecules opened out further until we were simply pure vibration, space, and movement. 'I' was no more. There was everything, and there was nothing. Eventually there was simply BEING – infinite Unity. I was less than a year old.

I believe we all experience something like this during the first year of life, but as soon as we start to identify 'other', and particularly when we begin to use language, this experience fades. But for some reason I never forgot. My world was a beautiful place of shifting colour and vibration rather than solid 'things'. It was a world where I could fly, vision, and shape-shift. I could read the thoughts and memories of people, animals, trees, furniture, and stones. I could 'see' with my hands. I could heal people and animals by moving energy through and around them. I could see events that had not yet happened. I experienced what seemed to be my past and future lives and deaths. I learned about magick, healing, and the nature of the universe from 'imaginary' friends – 'Mrs Grimble', 'Great Grandma Lilith', 'Shaman Healer Man', the 'E.T.s' and the 'Elders'.

These experiences have continued throughout my life. They have taught me to question everything, to never take my initial perceptions for granted, to look beyond the surface of apparent truth, to breathe into the silence for answers to my questions, and to trust my inner-sense. In my vibrational world I am One with everything. I belong. I know absolutely that I am loved – I feel it deep in my soul's connection with the universe. It is blissful. I know that, no matter what, I am always connected to everything else in the universe. I AM the world around me. I am all experience and I am all knowledge. I am pleasure and pain. I am celebration and sorrow. I am creation and destruction. I am life and death. I understand all of this as necessary aspects of nature and as aspects of myself. I also accept these as aspects of you. I therefore also love you for ALL that you are.

In my work as a teacher, healer, and therapist, people often come to me expressing their frustration at being unable to find any sense of connection and fulfilment. Many have a feeling that something fundamental is missing from their lives and that there should be 'something more'. I have devoted my life to the work of enabling these people to find their freedom, their ecstasy, their capacity for blissful healing love, and their 'something more'. I am also devoted to enabling _you_ to work towards personal empowerment, spiritual transformation, enlightenment, and joy.

I love you, because I am you.

Roots

Mysticism

There are many ancient and contemporary mystics, from all over this world and other worlds, who understand the forces of nature and the universe in the same way. They know of the process of transformation, creation, and manifestation – the power of magick. They have the understanding that the ALL (collective, universal energy) is a creative and transformative force. They understand that everything within nature vibrates with the same energy and is an aspect of the ALL. They therefore understand that everything, and everyone, is also a creative and transformative force and that the ALL is actually ONE – there is no division. The deeper truth of this 'reality' is so profound that becoming aware of it will transform your perception of everything, and therefore it will transform your reality. This wisdom brings personal divinity rather than the need for hierarchical power structures. Unfortunately for most, this knowledge has been lost (hidden) due to the uprising of organised, monotheist, religion.

Religion

It is important to note that when I discuss 'monotheist religion' throughout this book, I am referring mainly to the older, organised, civil, world religions which align themselves with politics and social control – such as

Christianity, Islam, and Judaism. My aim is to highlight the ways in which I believe these religious institutional bodies work to control cultures. I have no disagreement with individual devotees or followers of these religions who have found their salvation and are happy with their chosen path. Neither am I suggesting that every employee of these institutions is working from the same controlling principles – individual priests may even be unaware of the shenanigans of the upper echelons, and smaller or younger branches of these religions, that have split off from the main-stream, may work with much more of a focus towards individual fulfilment, often with a gentle and person-centred approach. So please bear this in mind when reading further.

Priests, politicians, and royals, in their hunger for power and riches, work together under the guise of holiness, rightness, and goodness. Although they are outwardly religious, it is not in their interest to openly offer the self-empowering knowledge of ancient spiritual wisdom. Instead they use their understanding of the power of ritual and belief creation, together with the threat of violence or punishment, to efficiently generate fear-driven followers, or (aptly named in the Bible) 'sheep'.

Knowledge of the value of personal freedom, empowerment, and divine connection is the untainted core of all spiritual practice – this is, in fact, written in all the spiritual texts. However, monotheist religions, and the societies they create, go to great pains to hide this. They have secretly encoded the true ancient wisdom within the stories of their holy books and within their rituals – it is all there if you know where and how to look. For example:

- The symbol of the separate, singular God, who is at the same time 'all things' and 'everywhere', misrepresents and confuses the idea of 'unity' consciousness. This also sets people up to believe that they are being watched and judged by an 'all-seeing' entity, bringing constant underlying anxiety into people's lives – it is impossible to experience personal divinity if you are in fear.
- Praying to God disguises the value of personal reflection (meditation) by ensuring that the quietened mind is diverted away from the wisdom of the inner world and towards the supposed religious teachings of an external deity.
- Encouraging the focus on the superficial stories of the holy books, rather than highlighting the hidden meaning within, ensures that people get drawn into the dramas, instead of the inherent wisdom.
- Their rituals are based on ancient, empowering, magickal wisdom, but they are performed only by the priests, who are placed carefully between the congregation and God – ensuring that the 'flock' simply watch from a distance rather than take an active role. This separates people from their divine consciousness, and perpetuates people's belief that they have no power of their own.
- The suggestion that sex is a sin that will lead people to the gates of hell ensures that the sexual experience is short and to the point (merely for making babies) – leaving no time to take pleasure, to breathe deeply, and to fully explore the process without guilt. This keeps people away from the path of personal divinity via the experience of ecstasy.

Monotheist religions decry all religions and spiritual practices other than their own. They also demonise everything that is associated with women: 'goddess', intuition, sex (including temple/sacred sex), menstruation, herbal medicine, the role of priestess or 'wise woman', and women's bodies in general – as their wisdom and skills are a particular threat to the patriarchal religious rule. In Europe, during the 13th to the 17th century, there was a period now known as the 'burning times'. During this time, estimates suggest, up to 9 million people, mostly women, were tortured, abused, imprisoned, and murdered by church assigned religious authorities for practicing the traditional and ancient ways known as witchcraft, or simply because of their gender or sexual orientation. Despairingly, this kind of thing is still happening today.

Many religions work to control beliefs and actions by eliciting fear, guilt, and shame. These feelings are generated by the manufacture of superstition, around 'correct spiritual practice' or 'right action', and the threat of judgement by an external, powerful, godly force – leading to punishment by hell realms, evil entities, or karma. The myths they tell, and their torturing/murderous actions, elicit such deep terror that people will follow any rule.

Over many thousands of years the mystical knowledge of the true, unifying, and therefore non-hierarchical, wisdom has been hidden within the highest echelons of these religions. Details of the extreme corrupt nature of the religious/political patriarchy are also hidden there. The 'All' or the 'One' came to be portrayed, not as abundant energetic life that is everywhere, but as a single god – an all seeing, all powerful individual. This gave huge power to the priests – who deemed themselves the only people worthy of understanding and communicating with this god. Their myths told of a place called 'heaven' where, if you behaved yourself, you could live in bliss – a tempting afterlife promising eternal happiness to which the priests held the key. People gave up their traditions, freedom, land, property, wages, rights, and choices in order to be 'saved' from what was quickly becoming a living hell – forgetting that the bliss was already within them.

Step onto Your Own Path

In my role as a teacher of spirituality, sacred sexuality, and mysticism, I repeatedly come across people who are struggling with a need to discover their true path, to express their own divine presence in this world, and to find their 'something more'. People often feel unhappy, they struggle with life's challenges, and they find themselves in battles with their families and friends. Many people feel that they are missing something, something deep, and they feel unfulfilled. Some people have turned to religion, others have sought the answer in the spirituality of other cultures (yoga, Buddhism and shamanism etc.), but many still find themselves frustrated as their deep need for spiritual connection remains unanswered.

By looking to a holy book or to other people/beings (gods, Buddha, Jesus, priests, shamans, masters, and gurus) for all the answers, and depending on them to tell you about what's right and wrong, how to behave, and who you should be, rather than discovering this wisdom yourself, you are giving up your own power. Unfortunately many of the priests, gurus, and holy books of religions and cults will ask this of you. You may lose sight of your intuitive wisdom, and the fulfilment you find may well be hollow.

Within the pages of the 'holy' books, and on communication with these 'enlightened ones', some wisdom can possibly be found. However, one would need to find a way through the maze of rules, superstitions, myths, dogma, and the egos' of these gurus in order to find anything nearing truth. Whenever it is suggested that someone or something other than you can bring you to unity, wisdom, truth, knowledge, or enlightenment be very suspicious. You may be left feeling even more confused after taking on new beliefs, and sometimes even new cultures.

Mystics are those who step deeply into themselves to discover their own empowering Truth and to seek a personal connection with the Divine All. Mystics discover through direct personal experience rather than through learned belief or the faith of religion. The ancient maxim 'know thyself' is their directing statement – as experiential self-knowledge leads to a knowledge of all the forces in the universe and, eventually, to a transformation of the soul. The practice of mysticism is aimed at training the body and the consciousness towards a state ready for the discovery of spiritual enlightenment. There are many different mystical paths. Magick is one of them.

Magick

Throughout this book I will be using the term 'magick'. The 'k' was added to distinguish it from stage magic. The word 'magick' has lost its original meaning and people generally meet it with superstition and fear. Even the magickal knowledge that was kept secret, and that has been slowly released over the last 400 years within small groups and publications, is confused with the beliefs of the prevailing religion and culture of the time. These influences have encouraged blind ritual, secrets, dogma, superstition, belief systems, hierarchy, and fear or worship of outside entities, even within current magickal practice. All of these are unnecessary and can be a barrier to the transformative process.

Without the unnecessary additions, magick simply means: transformation through unity – the art of creating change by unifying or aligning with the desired result. When we unite with All it is possible to transform anything.

A New Story

It is my goal to help you to reawaken the mystic within you and to aid in the rediscovery of your personal, ecstatic connection with the Divine through meditation and magick. In this book I offer you a practice which is accessible, simple, and untainted by superstition or belief in anything outside of your own personal experience. As a first step towards this I have written a story. Using the magickal tool of myth making, I will help you to experience the reality of mystical wisdom.

As I have said, monotheist religions use the same tools as magicians do. However, they use them to influence and control the collective belief system. They create myths and present them as truth in order to affect people's behaviour. 'Adam and Eve' and 'The Fall of Man' make up one of the most powerful, dangerous, and culturally influential Bible myths. It conceals ancient mystical wisdom and teaches people to fear knowledge. Whether your family is religious or not, if you were brought up in a monotheist culture, this story about the Garden of Eden has subliminally influenced you for your whole life.

However, I have rewritten this story and turned it on its head. Not only will it now enable you to have the experience of mystical wisdom, the new story exposes some of the secrets that the old story concealed. Also, while you take it in, it will work to repair some of the damage that the Bible story has left behind in your psyche.

A New Story

The story I have written also draws on early Sumerian, Babylonian, and Hebrew myths of the 'first woman' in the Garden of Eden. In these early stories 'Lilith' was created at the same time as Adam. They were made together, equally and of the same stuff, as manifestations of the divine spirit on Earth. In these stories Lilith was powerful and inquisitive. She refused to be a slave to Adam's sexual demands preferring a more empowered and equal expression of her sexuality.

When the male god of these stories realised the danger of this powerful, sexual, and creative woman, with all her wisdom and intuition, she was banished from the garden and punished. This story warns against people's (especially women's) attempts to stand up to the politics of the church, and it is a reminder to relinquish power to male husbands and priests. Lilith has since been omitted from any bible stories except as a demon. Eve was created to replace her. Made from Adam's rib, rather than from the earth like Lilith and Adam, the story of the gentle and subservient Eve puts women very clearly in their place.

The story I have written about the Garden of Eden is very different. Just like ancient Bible myths, I have written this story carefully and have used specifically placed symbolism. This story will deeply instil a very profound belief. However, unlike religious stories, this belief is not about control, and there is no fear-raising hidden agenda. It simply raises a belief in you that YOU are a powerful and magickal being. The only agenda here is to bring you to this understanding. This in turn will bring you closer to the discovery of your true ecstatic self, and closer, therefore, to your freedom from fear.

As you read the story, relax, take some slower deeper breaths, close your eyes, and meditate for a while before you begin. Give yourself time to take in the profound knowledge that is offered here. As you read the story and feel the powerful emotions it evokes, you will begin the work of undoing some of the fears that your unconscious has picked up throughout your life. As you read, breathe the emotions into your body. If it feels right for you, welcome this truth and this light, and use the magick in the story to transform and empower you – become Lilith. Become All.

Lilith Rising

There was once a beautiful garden. It was filled with abundant and limitlessly creative life, colourful exotic plants, and wild animals. The great All was reflected everywhere – in the deep green of the leaves, in the intoxicating perfume of the huge vibrant flowers, and in the radiant rainbow light that glowed from every living thing. There were many trees in this garden; two of these trees were particularly beautiful. They glowed and pulsated with a sparkle that reflected their special magick. One was called the Tree of Life and the other was called the Tree of Knowledge. When an animal ate the fruit of the Tree of Life they were given eternal life and health. When an animal ate the fruit of the Tree of Knowledge they came to understand the secret knowledge of All. Many had eaten of the Tree of Life but none had yet found the Tree of Knowledge.

Every animal had special skills or qualities that had arisen as a way to negotiate their world, to stay alive, to stay healthy, and to reproduce – some could blend into their environment by changing the colour of their skin, some had very long necks to reach fruits and leaves that were high up in the trees, and some had grown special feathers which they displayed to attract mates or to frighten off predators. Many types of animal lived in groups that worked as a team to gather food and protect each other. For these animals emotions and communication were particularly important skills – love, sensual touch, and physical pleasure helped them to develop strong bonds within their groups, anger helped them protect each other, and fear helped them escape from danger.

Human animals lived in groups and their special quality was 'thinking'. Many animals did this but, for humans, this skill had become a particularly important method of survival. They thought about everything they did – they attempted to understand their world by analysing and organising, they counted and measured everything, and they made up stories and created beliefs based on their conclusions.

In this garden were many human animals who lived together in large groups and loved each other. It was said that Adam and Lilith were the first to settle here in Eden. The two of them would sit together in the evenings, watching the sunset, and they would feel a deep connection with the beauty around them. They knew that, just by watching, they were an intrinsic element of this exquisite creation.

Adam and Lilith both had dark skin and shining black hair. Their eyes were clear and bright, and their faces had lines that suggested many years of smiles and laughter. Lilith had a curvy, soft body which was powerful and fit from playing, dancing, building, and collecting food. Adam was tall, and his long arms and legs were graceful and strong. He would love to run through the forests and the open spaces of Eden. The beauty of the radiant life here would touch him so deeply that he would often return from his run with his face wet from tears of joy that couldn't be held back.

Lilith Rising

As more people joined them in this beautiful country, Adam and Lilith would tell stories of the magickal quality of the life here. The people loved the stories. They would all sit together in the evenings listening to them, and retelling them, over and over again. The people found the idea of the collective creative intelligence comforting, and they felt it in themselves. They would celebrate the abundance and beauty of nature and the great All with rituals of dancing, singing, chanting, and love-making.

However as the communities became larger, and farming, rather than hunting and gathering, became more prevalent, food was experienced as scarce. In the past they would have simply moved to another area when food ran out. But now food would come and go depending on the weather and the time of year. People began to attempt to control the nature around them rather than live in harmony with it as they had done previously. As the fear of loss grew inside them they shared with each other less and less. The people began to feel powerless and vulnerable. It was during these times that they sometimes lost their ability to identify with the collective loving intelligence. People managed this loneliness in different ways – some simply carried on with their lives waiting for the wisdom to return, some searched for and found wisdom by transforming the pain, some believed that the joy was taken from them because they had done something wrong, and there were some who, in their pain, sought power and control over the others.

These power hungry people saw an opportunity. Due to their own fear of hunger, they wanted all the food and the land for themselves. They realised that people were easy to manipulate when they were frightened. They told the people that there was little point to their dancing, their chanting, and their reverence for nature – as the Earth was no longer abundant. They told the people that there was no collective intelligence, it was not everywhere, it was not in the Earth, and it was not in their bodies. Instead they told them that there was a single all-seeing god – a man who would watch them from above. They said that 'God' had put them in charge and they were now to be called 'priests'.

The priests ordered the people to follow them. They said that God would reward good behaviour but would also punish bad behaviour. They would prove their stories by connecting people's misfortune with a 'bad' behaviour they had done in the past. These priests said that if people wanted their lives to be enjoyable and safe again they must pay God in money, food, property, and penance. The old rituals, which revered the abundant Earth and the beauty of nature, were said to be evil and people were told that they would be punished if they continued with them. They were told to wear clothes that covered their genitals and that their love-making was now a 'sin'. The priests didn't want people to be reminded of their personal power to create. Women were said to be temptresses who, with their desires and their sexually appealing bodies, would lead the men away from their path of hard-work, penance, and abstinence. The people began to worry obsessively. Their thoughts were now fears upon fears about what might happen to them in the future and what they might have done wrong in the past. The 'Now' was forgotten.

Eventually, with the new quiet and sombre rituals, the constant fear, and the countless rules, the memory of the original stories faded. The joy of the present moment, the feeling of abundance, the dancing, and the communal love-making stopped. The divine was no longer experienced from within. All the qualities of the creative force of the universe were now bestowed onto this single external being. As the people learned fear, their joy for life faded.

If someone broke the rules it made the people feel angry and scared of God's rage. They tried to discourage each other from breaking the rules by telling stories of horrific punishment. If anyone made a mistake they became anxious and scared of this punishment – they felt guilty and feared discovery. They would try to talk to God and beg for forgiveness in the hope that God's anger would not be kindled. It was with great sadness that Lilith watched these changes come, and she began to feel very alone – even Adam began following the new rules – but, as the first woman, she never forgot the awe of their first days here in the Garden of Eden.

Lilith took to walking alone in the woodlands. She would enjoy this reconnection with the wildness of nature after being with the religious people and all their restrictions and control. She would dance naked and sing to the animals and the trees; she would enjoy her sensual and sexual body without guilt or shame. It was on one of these excursions that she came across the Tree of Knowledge for the first time. It drew her attention as it glowed with particular magnificence. The large red fruit, a kind she had never seen before, appeared succulent and tasty. Carefully, she picked one of the beautiful fruits and took a tentative bite.

Immediately her senses were overwhelmed by the pleasure of the honey-sweet sensation on her tongue. Her thoughts stopped. Her body stilled. In that moment all she knew was the sweet juice that filled her mouth and trickled down her chin and onto her breast. The silence filled her.

Lilith was held in an eternal moment of Now. It was a moment of deep knowing. Her whole being began to reach out to the infinite light all around her. Her heart opened, and she knew a love so complete that she fell to her knees – unable to stand while holding this experience of total fulfilment. Tears of joy streamed down her cheeks as her memories of Eden as it once was came flooding back.

She laid down on the ground, pressing her back into the soft grass and spreading her arms and legs wide, waiting and ready. As she opened to the experience and welcomed the light, Lilith began to feel waves of vibration coursing through her. She felt her physical body cracking open to release the infinite light that exploded from the depths of every part of her. The light expanded out in all directions – down through the Earth below her, out into the forest, and up into the sky above. Her whole body shook and convulsed as every muscle released into the ecstasy. She savoured the intensity of the experience with every part of her sensual and energetic being, and she released deep orgasmic roars that shook the forest.

She remained here for a long time afterwards, her body occasionally convulsing as further bursts of vibration were released. Eventually she stood up feeling taller, stronger, more beautiful, and more expansive than she'd ever felt. She knew that this joy and knowledge were not just for her. She was suddenly filled with the excitement of wanting to share this with her people so they too could remember.

As Lilith travelled back to her village she could feel herself changed. She was aware of herself, and everything else, as pure vibration. She experienced every moment as an act of creation. She moved through the shining light of the garden and the garden moved with her. As her mood lifted, her light, and the light of everything around her, brightened. The forest flowers turned their colourful heads and the trees reached their branches out towards her as she passed. These experiences revealed to her exactly how she created her own universe.

When she arrived at the home village and met with her family they looked upon her with suspicion – they could sense a change. To Adam, Lilith looked the same but she seemed different, more powerful. She told them all of profound love and beauty, of magickal power, and of deep connection with all things. Lilith was not surprised by their suspicion, but she continued with her joyful story. She expressed her realisation that she was the creative power of the universe and that they all were too. She told them of her understanding that there was no God to punish them – which meant that they were free to express their own truth. She reminded them that the rules they now believed in were based on fear and that there really is no good or evil – there is simply energy and experience. She told them that she received this knowledge from eating the fruit of a secret tree in the garden.

Her family were frightened – they did not understand the things that Lilith was saying. Her change felt like a threat and they refused to eat the fruit that she offered them. They had so much fear of the transformation in Lilith that they forced her to leave the tribe, and she was banished from Eden. They were so scared of change that they also decided to ban people from eating from the Tree of Knowledge – yet many of the other animals began feasting there.

Although they missed Lilith and were sad when she left, the people of Eden continued with their lives as they were. Adam met and fell in love with a different woman – her name was Eve. Eve was gentle and kind. Her dark hair was streaked with gold and it curled softly around her face, framing a smile that radiated love. She was always ready with open arms when someone needed to be held. She would cradle anyone with such a powerful and nurturing love that they felt deeply comforted. As the memory of Lilith faded, Eve took her place as the first woman.

Lilith spent many days, months, and years in the lands surrounding Eden. She explored the vibrational world – moving into and through the energy of All. She noticed how subtle changes in her own energy created changes in the energy around her. Each thought or feeling was accompanied by a shift of energy within herself and was reflected in the external environment. Each day she closed her eyes and silenced her thought. In these moments, she was able to join with the infinite and she would experience boundless and timeless ecstasy. The more she practiced this magickal act the more she met the infinite in her every experience. Her life was transformed. She learned to heal herself of any illness or pain she had ever had by finding its origin somewhere deep in her soul and transforming it with bliss. She began to regenerate herself as a being of life, of light, and of power.

Lilith spent time contemplating how she could finally bring the knowledge to the people of Eden. She wanted to set her people free because she loved them. She needed to get back, but she knew they wouldn't allow her in. However, her new knowledge had changed her experience of the world around her. During her time away from Eden she learned how to move as an energy-being and she learned how to create by focusing her thoughts. She knew now that her human form was not a physical structure that was able to think, but that it was a form that had come to be *because* of thought. She now understood that she was made of energy, thought, and memory. She knew that by changing her thought she was able to change her form. Over time, she developed this understanding of the universe to such a degree that her belief was strong enough to create any change she wanted. She practiced and practiced until she was able to appear as different animals and plants, or even rocks. Eventually, she chose a snake as her disguise in order to return to Eden.

As the snake, she was long and muscular. Her scales reflected the light as she meandered through the trees – a shimmering black mass winding her way home. As the snake, she entered Eden and passed through the gardens without notice making her way back to the Tree of Knowledge. When she arrived, she found that a large fence had been placed around the tree and the many apples that the tree had offered were scattered and rotting on the ground within the boundaries of the fence. Although this saddened her, she understood that the people had lost themselves to fear. She passed through the fence and worked her way up into the branches of the tree. Having settled herself, she released a thought "let the right person come to me". She waited.

In that very moment Eve stood up, not quite knowing why. She left the children she was tending to and headed out of the village and into the trees beyond. She walked through the woodland. She was not quite sure why she had set off on this journey but she found herself enjoying the rare moments of solitude. She soon came to be walking near the Tree of Knowledge. She recognised the fence that the people had put there and she also recognised the tree's peculiar but alluring luminescence. She stopped at the boundaries of the fence to enjoy the vision in front of her.

As she looked at the tree, she heard someone call her name. She stopped and looked around but could see no one. She heard her name again and realised that the call was coming from within the tree. With some fear she climbed carefully over the fence and stepped closer to the tree. She listened again. Her name was called once more. Stepping closer, she looked at the tree and soon noticed a glistening, thick, black snake wrapped around the lower branches. The snake was watching her.

Lilith called Eve again – her whispering snake-voice radiating love – and Eve began to feel safer and calmer. She sat down under the tree and looked up into the branches above her. She felt the luminous power of the tree and her body vibrated with anticipation of what, she somehow knew, was about to happen.

Lilith Rising

Lilith moved gently down the trunk and joined Eve. She coiled around Eve's body and allowed her own powerful vibrations to expand. Eve trusted instinctively. She closed her eyes and opened herself to receive these vibrations. She wanted to learn. She wanted to know. She breathed deeply into this moment experiencing the sensual and spiritual pleasure of pure connection with another. As her knowledge grew, Eve found herself able to give her own energy in return. Lilith and Eve moved and breathed together in a deeply sensual and ecstatic embrace – sharing all that they knew, sharing their bodies, and sharing their pleasure. Eventually, filled with joy and love for each other, they fell into dream realms together. While they journeyed there, Lilith showed Eve the magickal world that was all around her. She invited her to enter the boundless Oneness. Their rapture filled them as they joined the shimmering light.

They were One.

They were All.

After a long while of sleeping, sharing, and dreaming together, they awoke refreshed and energised. Eve immediately picked one of the tree's red, succulent fruits and took a drippingly delicious bite. Instantly her eyes were opened. She could no longer see the trees in the forest around her. She could only perceive energy – denser here, translucent there. She looked down at her own body. There was a vague memory of form but now she was simply made of shimmering light. She became aware of Lilith's light also and once again they danced together, this time a dance of infinite energy, moving around, through, and within each other.

Eve felt so much love she wanted to share it – she wanted to run to her people and tell of the wonder of the Tree of Knowledge. They began their journey together back to the village. Lilith returned to her human form and walked with Eve. While they walked, Lilith warned Eve of her experience with the people in the past. But they soon forgot this story. The people's fears and judgements were nothing to them now as they bathed in the magnificence of nature, knowing that all is as it should be. They moved with the universe.

They soon arrived at the boundaries of the village, and Lilith waited there. She radiated vibrations of love and understanding into the village. The people were happy to see Eve as she had been gone a while. Eve didn't speak. She simply smiled, held out her hand, and closed her eyes. A fruit from the Tree of Knowledge magickally appeared there. It reflected the sunlight on its shimmering red flesh. Some of the people recognised the fruit. Some of the people recognised Eve's magick. Many screamed in fear and ran away. "You will be punished!" they cried as they ran. The others looked on with suspicion.

Adam came when he heard the screams. He saw Eve holding the fruit. She looked radiant and he felt his love for her. "This fruit will bring you all knowledge." Eve spoke gently. "It will set you free to be your powerful truth. It is your choice – to eat and be awakened or to remain as you are." In this moment Adam remembered Lilith – the time they had shared together in the beginning of Eden, and her sad departure. Hearing the truth in Eve's words but knowing that, as a woman, she would be mistrusted by the people, Adam offered to speak to them. Eve understood and agreed.

"I will eat of the Tree of Knowledge because I was offered it once before by my first love, Lilith. I saw the beauty of her truth but I denied myself this knowledge because I was frightened of the god we had made. Now another woman I love is telling me the same. This time I will be fearless. I will choose to join Eve in this abundant light." He took a bite from the apple, and instantly he felt the transformation. He smiled. The plants and trees reflected him with joyful energy. The power of his loving smile was returned to him a hundred times over. After a long sigh, he spoke again. "I remember that the real story of the divine is not the one we now tell. The great All is the fulfilment, the power, the joy, and the love within each of us. There is no necessity for fear, anger, or punishment. Every one of you is perfect. You don't need to be anything other than who you are."

Eve was grateful for Adam's support. After seeing the effect of the apple on Adam, the people began to feel safer. They came towards Eve and looked deeply into her radiant eyes. They could see the integrity there, and they began to trust. They asked her questions, they listened, and they learned as she sat with them and shared her wisdom.

In his bliss, Adam became aware of Lilith's powerful energy radiating from the trees and he walked over to greet her. They embraced and kissed deeply, and immediately felt their deep connection and love for each other. Adam wondered at the immense and unconditional love she was capable of which enabled her to see beyond such cruel treatment from her family. He thanked Lilith for working so relentlessly to bring the knowledge back to the people, and he expressed his grief and regret for his personal rejection of her. They held each other, moving and breathing together, and they made-love once again – one body, one spirit, locked in an eternal ecstatic moment. As they lay together, Adam remembered – he knew that nothing mattered but the fulfilment, the healing, and the love that Oneness brings. Eventually, Lilith and Adam turned their attention back to the excitement in the village.

It seemed that some of the other people also wanted to understand. Eve had created more and more apples for them. Adam and Lilith watched as people ate them. One-by-one they experienced the infinite joy of universal love, as they joined with the vibrations of life around them. Some of the people who had initially run away were cautiously returning. Eve continued to hand out apple after apple, as more of the people in the group became illuminated. Adam and Lilith walked over to join them. They laughed and shared long, deep, knowing gazes with the radiating eyes of the people. They embraced and kissed Eve with a depth of sensual and all-encompassing love that only comes from truly knowing another's divinity. They were free once again.

This is a true story.

Take some time to breathe and relax before you read on.

The Old Stories

Original 'Sin'

The story of the Garden of Eden also appears in both The Koran and The Torah. There are some differences in each portrayal therefore I will focus specifically on the Bible story. The second chapter of Genesis in the Old Testament (Adam and Eve and the Fall of Man) is a story that has brought about a deeply-rooted fear of knowledge and power. This story includes the myth of 'the original sin', in which a woman disobeys the words of God. This myth consolidated the misogyny which already prevailed in early monotheist religion.

In the story, God made a garden filled with trees that were 'beautiful and good for food'. God formed Adam in 'his' own image out of the dust of the ground. In the middle of the Garden of Eden were the 'Tree of Eternal Life' and the 'Tree of the Knowledge of Good and Evil'. Adam was commanded by God not to eat from the Tree of Knowledge, on pain of death, but was encouraged to continue to eat from the Tree of Eternal Life.

God decided that Adam needed a 'helper' and 'companion'. So while Adam was sleeping, God took one of his ribs and made a woman from it. Adam named her 'woman' because she was 'taken out of man' (note, not the other way around).

There was a 'crafty' serpent who came and told the woman that she wouldn't die if she ate from the Tree of

I Am God

Knowledge but that her eyes would be opened instead, she would become 'like God – knowing good from evil'. When the woman saw that the fruit of the tree brought wisdom and enlightenment, she took some and ate it. She also gave some to Adam. They then had knowledge of 'good' and 'evil' and became 'aware of their nakedness' i.e. their 'tools' of creation.

When God discovered this, he cursed the woman – 'increasing her pain both in childbirth and in her monthly blood' (menstruation came to be known as 'the curse') and by telling her that she would be 'ruled by her husband'. Adam was punished because he 'listened to his wife' and he was made to work the land until he returned to it in death. In the story, God says that now 'man' has knowledge 'he' must become mortal otherwise he will become 'like one of us' (divine). God also cursed the serpent to crawl on its belly and eat dust for the rest of its life.

This teaches people that:

- ❖ God is a male who makes, controls and can destroy everything.
- ❖ Man is made in the image of God.
- ❖ Woman is made from the body of man.
- ❖ The reason for women's existence is to be 'helper' and 'companion' to men.
- ❖ It is dangerous for a man to listen to a woman.
- ❖ It is dangerous to go against the word of God.
- ❖ It is dangerous to break rules or poke around in forbidden places – if you do, terrible things will happen.

The Old Stories

- ❖ It is dangerous to listen to your intuitive wisdom (symbolised by the serpent).
- ❖ Humankind is 'cursed' because of the temptations of a woman.
- ❖ It is dangerous to 'eat from the tree' – i.e. to have knowledge.
- ❖ Knowledge brings pain, suffering, and continual work and knowledge is 'evil'.
- ❖ With knowledge you understand 'nakedness' (sex) – that is, you know of your ability to <u>create</u> life, you can experience ecstatic states, and you can therefore become like God.
- ❖ It is dangerous to become like God.

What the Bible states very clearly is that the knowledge is plainly there, available right in front of you, and that you *can* become like the creator by simply 'eating' of the Tree of Knowledge. But it warns you against it over and over again. These messages keep people from their own knowledge, power, and divinity, and they have become the blueprint for our behaviour and social structure.

The Myth of Woman as Demon

The god of monotheistic religion was not only singular, it was also seen as male – like the priests. The world was divided. Everything commonly (and falsely) associated with 'male' (physical strength, focused thinking, competitiveness, domination, assertiveness and unemotional/rational decision making) was also associated with God (good, normal, right, powerful, valuable, light, positive, and divine). We can see the reflection of this in our language even today. Words that describe men are acceptable, fun, or powerful whereas words for women which describe exactly the same concept are seen as unacceptable, wrong, scary, and laughable. Compare the following:

wizard, bachelor, stud, priest, dick

witch, spinster, slag, priestess, cunt

Everything which isn't male-like is not God and is therefore seen as evil, bad, dirty, dark, negative, dangerous, wrong, and weird. Not-God is: demon, evil, woman, animal, menstruation, emotion, gentleness, softness, carer, mother, priestess, midwife, healer, witch, intuition, psychic vision, and goddess. Goddesses have been demonised, and made into evil or destructive forces – for example, Kali, Hecate, and of course Lilith – creating fear around the power of the feminine, or they have been desexualised. For example, the symbol 'Virgin Mary' of Christianity removes all sexual power whatsoever. This informs and encourages misogyny and the abuse of women. It informs the misuse of male power and the negation of everything feminine – men who allow emotion or gentleness are often ridiculed. It upholds the myth that men are stronger, more capable, and in charge – albeit under the watchful eye of a vengeful god.

Messages of wicked witches, nasty step mothers, sexual predators (bunny boilers), and subservient women who depend on men in order to survive, are not only perpetuated via religion and its supporters (politics and the education system) they are maintained via the seemingly innocuous avenues of fairy tales, advertising, and entertainment. The messages are also supported in the judicial system where women are often punished more heavily than men for the same crimes or where crimes such as burglary or tax evasion are met with more severe sentences than sexual or violent crimes against women. The messages are also sustained in the very structure of our culture, where men generally hold the most 'important' and 'powerful' jobs and the work that women tend towards is underpaid and undervalued.

The Culture of Control

Myth is an incredibly powerful and transformative magickal process which uses symbol and emotive content to implant ideas deep into your unconscious. Used consciously and with the right intention it can bring joy and expansion of being. In the wrong hands, and with dangerous stories, myth perpetuates fear and limits self-realisation. It has been used in this way by religious/political organisations to influence, manipulate, and control cultures.

The 'original sin' is the story we have all been told. It is the prevailing myth we live under. Even if you haven't been brought up in a religious family, this myth and others have influenced the blueprint from which you manifest your reality, and this gives rise to your thoughts, beliefs, judgements, and perceptions about yourself, others, and the environment around you.

It may seem like a simple story but the symbolic power of The Garden of Eden is more far reaching than you'd ever imagine. It is dangerous and power-stripping to all genders. It forces people into unnatural and disempowering gender-based dualistic roles within society and within relationships. By maintaining this environment of fear, all humans are separated from their right to freely express themselves in a way that is true and fulfilling. This ultimately disempowers and enslaves all but those who hold the reign.

A Disempowering Leadership

The monotheistic teachings encouraged separation from the collective ALL. The universal creative force became personified into this single all-seeing, judgemental, angry, and punishing father-figure. This was a very frightening mix that had the effect of keeping control over large cultures by maintaining an environment of perpetual fear. Understood to be the word of God in written form, the Old Testament actually encourages the murder and torture of any individual who is knowledgeable or powerful, or who differs in opinion or action.

The practice of marginalizing, killing, and punishing people who have different beliefs appallingly continues throughout the world today. Rather than empowering individuals with ancient teachings of personal transformation and enlightenment, these holy books are little more than instruction manuals for personal disempowerment and global violence. It is not surprising that cultures are warring and individuals live in judgement, hate, and fear of themselves and others when these teachings are at their foundation.

The Old Stories

Although you may not attend church services, align yourself with a particular religion, or read their publications, the stories, myths, rules, and fears propagated by religious organisations may still have a powerful influence over you. Cultures dominated by monotheist religion and its myths have worked to maintain a particular power structure, which disempowers the majority of individuals through its stories and threats. Even today, we are continually subject to consistent subliminal reiteration of the culturally-agreed messages via the media – regarding frameworks of good/bad, right/wrong, true/false, real/not real, and valid/invalid. If we are to become peaceful, loving, and enlightened beings, it is important to get below the surface of the accepted reality and find the truth hidden deep within.

Secrets

Apart from power and control, the priests were also hiding important knowledge with their stories:

- ❖ The knowledge that All is One.
- ❖ The knowledge that _we_ are the Creatrix.
- ❖ The knowledge that we are deserving of the bliss of Oneness and fulfilment.
- ❖ The knowledge that all genders, cultures, sexualities, abilities, and ages are equally valuable, powerful, and worthy of fulfilling their chosen paths.
- ❖ The knowledge that everyone has the ability to understand, experience, and benefit from the truth of Unity.

- ❖ The knowledge that we have all the wisdom already within us and we don't need to look outside ourselves in order to find it.
- ❖ The knowledge that, with training, our bodies and minds can be a conduit for the ecstatic state and therefore for divine creation.
- ❖ The knowledge that the structures and belief systems they have created are <u>entirely false</u>.

When you know their secrets you are no longer reliant on their religious, political, and social structures and you are free to live your life according to your true journey.

Steps to Change

Illuminate Yourself

The story of Lilith Rising is based on truth. It is absolutely possible to experience reality in the same way as Lilith. It is true that your reality is being created with every breath and every thought. It is true that you can move through your universe feeling absolute love and fulfilment in every moment. It is true that I am God and it is true that you are too.

How different do you imagine life would be if we had been offered a Garden of Eden story like the one written here as a foundation for belief and understanding? I suggest that you read this alternative story again and again – once or twice a day for many weeks. Change the names and genders around if it helps you identify with the main character. Read the story as if it were you. Let it become your new belief – a belief in yourself – and return to your divine right. Let this empowering message become your foundation. Notice what happens; notice how your life changes.

Becoming free involves a process of stepping out of disempowering belief systems and discovering your own personal reality. This can be daunting, as, in the process, you will become different from the people around you and therefore possibly unacceptable to many. You could give them the story to read to help them understand your changes. Or you could learn to bypass your ego's influence – as your fears about acceptance create feelings of anxiety within you, breathe the anxiety away, remind yourself that you are safe and that you are loved, and remember the Oneness. Rather than looking to culture, society, friends, and family for guidance, learn to look within. With careful handling, the ego's fears will eventually quieten and, instead of simply surviving, you will learn how to really live fearlessly. You will become true, and you will be free.

Are you Ready to Bite the Apple?

In this book you will find a map of your personal, mystical journey. It will give you the tools to discover divine connection for yourself and to find the pure essence of your spiritual being – free of religious interference. *I Am God* helps you to develop the skills to reach deep within yourself and open to the wisdom that you will find there. You will learn by going directly to your source – no gurus, no masters, and no priests.

The rituals and initiations offered here may not be unfamiliar as they are also offered via religion and other spiritual teachings – meditation, visualisation, astral travel, connection to nature, body work, altered states of consciousness etc. These practices were once the foundation of religious practice but the lessons within have been camouflaged by the myths that now surround them.

This book offers a reintroduction of our ancient mystical heritage – stripped of all unnecessary rules, superstition, dogma, and belief. I have worked to rediscover the source that lies at the root of all spirituality. This enables you to set out on a pure and clear path to your own knowledge and wisdom. The practices offer tools to inspire your spiritual experience and awaken you to the power and the delights of magick. You can then transcend the illusion of the boundaries of the physical world and gain knowledge of the Infinite. Your magickal experience will show you to be a microcosmic reflection of the divine. You will have opportunities to experience your boundless soul. You may become aware of your perfection and your full potential, enabling you to step onto the path of living your truth in the physical world – free from fear and pain. You may even develop the capacity to self-heal and to love without condition. The practices will show you that you don't need to connect with any religion or any god to become an enlightened soul capable of giving and loving. You need only to connect with the Divine Power that is the essence of who you are – the Truth that is YOU in every moment.

How to Use this Book

Each lesson takes you further out into the cosmos and, at the same time, deeper inside yourself and deeper into the now. You will benefit if you take the lessons in order as each exercise calls on the knowledge you have gained in the last. You may repeat each exercise as often as necessary until you feel ready to move on to the next. When you have finished everything, you can go back and redo any of the exercises as often as you like and in any order. Repeating exercises will always bring new knowledge, new insight, and new growth. You can also practice alongside a friend, a partner, or in a group. Comparing experiences and supporting each other is invaluable. You may be surprised at the amazing similarity of some of your experiences.

I have given a detailed explanation of the usefulness and the reason for each exercise or ritual. It is important that you know and understand everything before you go ahead. Blindly following instruction is a disempowering process.

Journal – your Personal Sacred Text

It is beneficial to keep a journal as you work through this book. Write, draw, and reflect on your experiences of the exercises and rituals and on your dreams and any day-to-day changes that you notice. Write down your thoughts, feelings, memories, visions, and inspirations. It is in this journal, and through your own wisdom, that you will find your own personal spiritual text. Refrain from attempting to label, make up meaning about, or interpret your experiences. This can limit the affects of the work. You don't need to understand what is happening consciously. Trust that your unconscious will do all that is necessary and it will go much deeper in its healing than your mind can ever take you.

Experiences of Be-coming

Your only goal is to become aware of your Divinity and accept your greatness, therefore coming into alignment with the truth of who you are. When you arrive at this point you will feel the sense of fulfilment, enlightenment, and love that you have been searching for and you will be ready to fulfil your life's purpose. This journey takes persistence and daily practice. The transformation may not be a wholly pleasant experience. You will be asked to look at parts of yourself that you have avoided. As you walk the

Steps to Change

path of experience, through the exercises in this book, you will notice great change. This will be rewarding but it may also be challenging. The techniques work to bring about growth and spiritual development and will begin the work of the natural homeostasis of the body and mind (the innate healing capacity). In order for these things to happen you may experience many new or previously unknown things about yourself.

This work can elicit the resurfacing of long forgotten memories. You may also experience a 're-viewing' of past events, particularly traumatic ones, as your psyche works to heal itself. You may find yourself crying or laughing for no apparent reason or engulfed in deep rage, grief, or ecstasy. These are all normal stages of development, and the release is helpful to your transformation. You may want to find a therapist to support you if you feel concerned.

As you continue in this work, the friends you currently have may struggle to understand who you are becoming as you begin to live your own truth rather than the truth that others expect of you. The environment around you will begin to look different as your perspective changes. You may also begin to notice energies that you have not previously been aware of, for example the auras or electromagnetic energy that surrounds people and things. You will experience more synchronicity, telepathy, and psychic experience, i.e. an intuitive 'knowing' about things, people, and events.

This is just a normal awakening of your brain's full potential brought on by the work that you are doing. These abilities have always been a part of you but you perhaps haven't noticed them before. However this isn't the goal, this is just a (positive) side effect of opening up the psyche. You are simply reawakening the skills that human animals have become separate from. Enjoy the experiences and integrate them as part of who you are. See them as a sign that you are progressing well. Know that all these things are steps in the right direction.

Now, let's begin...

Lilith Speaks:

I am goddess, priestess, witch, wisdom seeker, sacred whore, mystic, shaman, magician, seer, healer, and teacher.

I am all women, and all that is hidden, marginalised, and suppressed in any gender.

I had the courage to eat of the sacred Tree of Knowledge and, through ecstasy and inner wisdom, I remembered the secrets of the ancients, and re-united with my own divinity. I stepped through the gates of what was called 'heaven' — right here on Earth. I became God — creator, healer, All.

I was banished for thousands of years because I knew! I knew that my desirable, sensual, animal body, my words, and my thoughts were conduits for divine ecstatic creation. I was banished for my intuition and my wisdom, for speaking my truth, and for refusing to bow down to sexual slavery. I was banished for revealing their lies. They hid me, they demonised me, and they blamed me for all the pain and hurt that became the human experience.

I was the first woman — a hated example to you all. Their manipulation made you hate yourself too. You have learned to believe that your sensual and sexual body is the gateway to their hell. You have learned to hide your wildness, your passion, your innate wisdom, and your intuitive knowledge. You have learned to hide your voice and your truth behind a false half-reflection of yourself.

I cannot be silent any longer. I speak of ancient magick, rituals, and practices which will help you to free yourself from the physical, emotional, spiritual, psychological, and sexual slavery that you have unwittingly consented to.

I speak not only to women but to people of all genders who have been bullied into bowing down to outside control, taught to disbelieve their own inner wisdom, and forced to modify their behaviour in order to please others. Everyone suffers because of these thousands of years of religious manipulation.

To be divine is to be true. To be true we must learn to be wild again, to un-domesticate ourselves, to let go of all fear and self-hatred, and to uncover our true resonance with All that is.

You (whatever your gender) are beautiful, wise, and knowledgeable.

You are capable of more than you could ever imagine, and you can be free to express your truth without apology. It is time to stand up, step into your body, and roar your wild song into being!

I worship you as the embodied divine being that you truly are.

I am God and so are you.

1

Step

Into

Awareness

1 - Step into Awareness

Meditation – The Core Practice

The first step in personal transformation is meditation. The ability to clear the mind and become aware is a prerequisite to all successful mystical practice. For thousands of years mystics have known that it is in the inner silence that we connect with our divine self. It is the most important tool of transformation and enlightenment.

Meditation is not just a technique from the exotic East, that was picked up on the hippy trails of the 60's, it has always been an integral part of any mystical practice anywhere in the world and it has its roots in ancient civilizations. It is a practice that has been shared throughout all religions, cultures, and spiritual traditions in many different forms for thousands of years. Throughout history, different meditation techniques have been used to focus and clear the mind – from simple personal prayer to chanting and dancing in a tribal gathering.

Some traditions or religions insist that only specific meditations are useful or that you must wear particular clothes or meditate at a particular time or place for it to be worthwhile. But meditation is simple, you don't need to follow a belief system, it is free, and you already have all the equipment necessary. The meditations offered in this book are free of religion and dogma – you will be able to use this wonderful transforming tool without having to join any groups or believe in any guru or god. You need only to believe in yourself.

What is Meditation?

Meditation is the practice of awareness. It usually involves closing the eyes and sitting quietly, but many forms of meditation can involve the moving body, open eyes, chanting, or visualising. The basic steps of meditation are simple but not necessarily easy – just like anything you wish to be good at, you need to practice regularly.

- ❖ The first step is to wake up to the voices in your mind and the sensations in your body.
- ❖ The second step is to learn to notice these internal meanderings without reacting to them.
- ❖ The third step is to learn to be aware of the silence behind this chatter – the gap in thought.
- ❖ The fourth step is to enter this silence and expand your being into it.

These stages come when you are ready. They may come and go. You may find yourself expanded into the great blissful All one minute and in the next you will have popped back into mind-chatter mode. All these examples are stages of successful meditation.

It is unhelpful to chase any particular experiences as this will always lead you back to the chatter. Just watch the experiences come and go and try not to be attached to any of them. When meditating, although you feel very relaxed, you should also feel very clear, centred, alive, and awake to the present moment. It is an active rather than a passive process.

1 - Step into Awareness

Transformation & Healing

Meditation is helpful in many ways. It is well known that meditation has the effect of calming, relaxing, and quietening the mind. However, these are only small and somewhat superficial values of meditation. A major work of meditation is this:

*

When your thoughts are quiet, your deeper consciousness has the opportunity to repair itself.

*

Why does an aspiring deity need to do this?

Enlightenment is hindered by the anxieties of the everyday mind. The struggles created by past trauma create fears which limit your expression and therefore limit access to an expanded consciousness. During times of trauma or moments of intense fear the survival mechanism in the brain/body experiences a threat to life, and as a result lays down a deep information pathway. From this point on, whenever you are in a similar situation, your brain will trigger you into a feeling of anxiety. However, you probably won't realise that the present feeling is connected to the past experience.

For example, if a child was walking through a forest and was surprised by a wild boar behind a bush the pathway written in the brain might be: bush = danger. From this point on the child might have a fear reaction every time they pass this or any bush.

Another example – if a child is shouted at by a parent for interrupting a conversation the pathway written in the brain might be: interruption = danger. From this point on the child might have a fear reaction every time they need to interrupt their parent, or any person, and may avoid interruptions in the future. Something to note is that young children can experience their parents' disapproval as <u>life threatening</u>. One of the survival tactics of the child therefore is to fit in with the tribe or family. As children we learn the rules of acceptable behaviour and mould our expression accordingly.

Over time, the impact of small one-off experiences begins to fade. But if the same scenario is repeated, or if the scenario causes injury or pain, the pathways become more powerful and continue to direct our behaviour and our experience of situations over many years. Without healing, these pathways can remain for life. They act as filters through which we experience the world. This human survival mechanism is known by many names – including: ego, false-self, and child-self. From now on, I will mostly refer to it as 'little-you' as many of the pathways (not all) are laid down in childhood and the feelings evoked are often very childlike.

Little-you has one goal: to avoid immediate pain (death) and to move towards immediate pleasure (life). It cannot delay gratification – little-you will not be able to tolerate a small amount of pain in order to gain a better result for the future. This results in repeated unhelpful patterns of behaviour – for example, staying in a difficult relationship when you know you would be happier out of it. Here, the survival mechanism works to avoid the immediate pain of

1 - Step into Awareness

ending. When your behaviour is being directed via this part of your mind, i.e. when you are living as little-you (which for most people is most of the time), you will try to avoid being seen as bad, wrong, or unacceptable. This fear response is very limiting.

Little-you tells you to:

- Say 'yes' when you mean 'no' or say the answer you think people want to hear.
- Fit in and be acceptable so you will be loved and cared for.
- Smile when you would prefer to express something more real.
- Panic if someone says something that describes you as wrong or bad.
- Dress in a way that evokes approval from your peers.
- Panic if someone you love gives their attention to something or someone else.
- Avoid any perceived danger.
- Lie or pretend all the time.

These pathways, fears, and subsequent limited self-expression may have been useful during childhood – in order to be liked and therefore cared for by the parents – but for adults they are wholly unnecessary. As adults, in a non-tribal culture, we actually no longer need to rely on the approval of others in order to survive.

*
Most adults are still living and behaving according to their childhood fears!
*

If a trauma happens in adulthood the same process takes place – a fear pathway is laid down and from then on any similar situation can become a trigger. This also leads to limited expression due to fear and anxiety. One-off adult trauma is relatively easy to recover from. However, if there were also repeated childhood traumas, a trauma in adulthood can deepen pathways which already exist. It could even lead to the uncovering of forgotten childhood memories and act as a trigger to a major emotional crisis.

Because human animals are so busy thinking, fearing, and being distracted by work, TV, drugs, alcohol, and personal dramas, these past traumas get tucked into corners of the mind and/or the body. These suppressed memories not only direct our behaviour but they also can reappear in a variety of ways: physical twitches, irritability, over/under-eating, depression, anger, self-hatred, violence, anxiety, self-sabotage, addictions, 'accidents', and mental and physical health issues.

We falsely believe that our reactions of anger, fear, and sadness, and our reactive thinking, such as "I'm scared that they don't like me" or "you don't care about me enough", are created by a current situation. However, these unhelpful thoughts and feelings are *always* re-actions or a *re-enactment* of something that happened in the past that we are projecting into the here and now.

Do you hear that? ALWAYS!

In every moment (other than when there is immediate physical danger) that you are feeling anything other than

1 - Step into Awareness

calm happiness, or equanimity, you are re-acting due to past trauma.

<u>As an adult, you CREATE your reality based on what's happened before. You experience everyone as if they are your parent, your teacher, your attacker, your bully, or your abuser, and you are experiencing yourself as a child/victim.</u>

To become free from the fear and limitation caused by the past the very first and most important step is to work at healing, and eventually clearing, these pathways. This has to be continually worked at – <u>the pathways won't go away on their own</u>, and, until they do, you are stuck in the 'little-you' world of anxiety fuelled living which is far from the divine being that is lost underneath all of that.

*

Meditation does this work for you.

*

During regular meditation, while your mind is still and the thoughts and fears are quiet, your innate self-healer will go to the places where the triggers were set down and dig them out. With regular practice you will become more open and aware, even during the times when you are not meditating. During these increasing times of awareness you may be required to stop and give attention to the memories that have been unearthed. You will hear the words and feelings that little-you has been waiting to express. You might find yourself inspired to paint, write, rant, scream, sob, or grieve. In my many years of practice I have had various experiences of this spontaneous healing process. I will share a couple of examples to illustrate.

The first example came when I was aged 17. I was walking and chatting with a friend when suddenly my mind was filled with a memory that I had completely hidden from myself up until then. It was the memory of a big and somewhat shocking event in my life – one that I might have held negative judgements about, pre-meditation. However, due to the practice, I was able to accept and integrate this memory as part of my valuable life experience.

The second example came during a period of intense meditation practice (between six and eleven hours each day). During the rests between the two hour long meditation sessions my mind showed me the two most traumatic memories of my life. I was able to watch the details, like a mind-movie, and re-live them, but with a sense of distance and curiosity. While I watched, tears streamed from my eyes and deep sobs shook me. I wasn't feeling traumatised by the witnessing of these 'memory movies', it was a physical reaction of grief in the very pit of my stomach. By the time the 'movies' were finished (each one took about half an hour) I felt free of the burden of these experiences. I felt lighter, clearer, and happier.

During moments of trauma your mind is filled with new and often frightening information and experience. At some point soon afterwards it would be valuable to integrate and heal from these events. However, due to the fact that our minds tend to be full of work, worries, and entertainment, we don't often allow ourselves time to heal. Regular meditation practice gives time for this.

1 - Step into Awareness

The above are examples of the healing process which occurs during periods in your life when you are regularly meditating. During this process, give yourself deep love and understanding. Only then will you be able to clear the pathways. You may also want to consider therapy or other support as you are going through this process. If blocked memories do emerge it may be shocking for you. Although I have found that with regular meditation practice things emerge only when you are ready and able to deal with them. Although it may be challenging at times, if you continue your meditations the challenge should be manageable, as the meditation practice trains you to relax rather than re-act.

Meditation helps you to become a <u>real adult</u>. It brings you back to your power, and it enables you to really, deeply love yourself and other people without condition or need. Through regular practice you will learn new habits of thought and reaction. During meditation you are asked to watch without reacting. You will watch your thoughts come and go; you will watch sensations come and go. When you practice simply watching without responding during meditation, your mind will be trained to also remain present when you are not meditating, and you will begin to feel free of the re-active cycle. When you pay attention to your little-you thoughts, it can no longer run the show. You will change the habits that were started in childhood – you will be able to simply watch your unhelpful thoughts, smile, and carry on while feeling calm and happy – living in harmony with all that life brings.

It can be an exhilarating process, and it can be deeply challenging. Little-you will fight against the changes and attempt to sabotage your practice as it starts to panic. All the conditioned responses were there to protect you in childhood and these changes can feel like death. In fact a part of you *is* dying – your false identity/the little-you/the part of you that pretends in order to be acceptable. As your false identity begins to fall away you may wonder who, in fact, you are. The little-you might attempt to push you into a new identity that superficially seems to fit better with your new practice. For example, joining a 'spiritual' group and dressing, acting, or even eating in a similar way to the others in the group. This is still false. By doing this you are still conforming in order to be accepted by a group and you are not being true according to your deeper self.

These groups often have shared righteous delusions such as 'we've made it' and even 'we're so much better than others'. Look out for this kind of behaviour as it is a common side effect. You may well find yourself choosing different environments and sometimes different people to be around as you begin to change. This is normal for a person who is transforming. As long as you continue with your daily meditation practice you will notice any behaviours that are false in you, including newly developed false-identity behaviour, and they too will begin to naturally fall away. As you continue your development, you will stop wondering who you are and you will begin to simply be – without judgement, criticism or analysis of yourself or others.

Ah... freedom.

Expanded Consciousness

By now you are probably coming to realise that the first work of the aspiring deity is transformation of the self – from the fear driven little-you to a loving, truth-driven being who lives according to a deeper inner wisdom. However, meditation not only brings self-knowledge and transformation, it will eventually enable you to open to the collective consciousness giving you access to all knowledge – past, present, and future. It brings you to meetings, and ultimate union, with the boundless-oneness. This experience opens you to self-love and, eventually, to unconditional love for all. You will come to realise that the answers to all your questions are not in the outside world – in books, newspapers, from gurus, spiritual texts, etc. You will understand that the answers to everything lie deep within. Spiritual texts are merely descriptions, interpretations, and symbols of other people's experience of the divine. Your personal spiritual text is within you and meditation offers a journey to find it.

Intuition

Meditation develops the intuition. The unconscious remembers all the books you have ever read, every experience, every conversation, and every taste, sound, smell, image, and sensation. I believe that we also remember every experience that everybody and everything *else* has ever had and ever will have – this is often called the collective consciousness. Intuition is the ability of your mind to reach into your unconscious, and the collective consciousness, and pick out exactly the right information at the right time.

The only way you can connect with this information is if you connect with yourself and learn to listen to the subtle messages that come via your intuitive impulses. The unconscious speaks with symbols, subtle images, feelings and hunches. When you begin to pay attention, your unconscious will learn that you are attempting to listen, and the more you respond the more it will trust you with information. Meditation will help you do this.

Psychic Ability

With more meditation practice, you may begin to experience visions or see 'auras' – the life energy around living things. You may also experience amazing synchronicities and telepathic moments. These are all normal functions of the human brain which, over time, we have lost the capacity for. Having these experiences simply means that you are opening up your psyche – coming into contact with your natural abilities and using the parts of your brain function that have previously been closed down. But remember that these skills are only the beginning of your work towards personal transformation not the goal. If you continue with your daily practice the rewards will be even greater.

1 - Step into Awareness

Breath – Beginning and End

Your experience of the environment outside the womb begins with the first breath and your last exhale will herald the end. Although breath is a natural function which happens automatically without need for interference from your conscious mind, there is great value in developing an awareness of the breath. Your breath is affected by everything you do. Of course you are aware of your breath changing when you exercise, but do you notice changes when you are tense, stressed, anxious, or scared? Do you notice how your breath is affected by a rainbow, a beautifully wrapped gift, or the sight of a newborn child? Also, in reverse, the rhythm of your breath can affect your mood. If your breathing is too shallow due to habitual patterns it can cause a mild feeling of anxiety leading to a perpetuation of past fears.

Your journey towards the discovery of your personal divinity begins where you are right now with an exploration of the world that is your immediate experience – the universe within you. Your breath will lead you there. Breath is the most profound key to your life, your health, your being, and your truth. The following exercise will bring awareness to the breath. It is important that you don't try to change anything consciously. Try not to judge or analyse. Trust that your body will find the most helpful way without the interference of the mind. As you meditate, things will fall into place naturally. If anything is wrong the meditation will heal it. Trust your unconscious to use its innate wisdom towards healing.

For all of the following meditations use a timer with a gentle alarm. This will allow you to focus fully rather than having to stop to check the time. If you don't need to concern yourself about things on the outside you can enter much deeper states of consciousness. Read through the exercise a few times before you begin in order to become familiar with it.

Sit in a relaxed but upright posture, either in a chair or on the floor. Try to keep your spine straight (not tense) and free from restrictions. Try not to lean against anything in order to allow the energy in your body to move freely and to stop yourself falling asleep. This position may be uncomfortable or painful at first, but it is worth persevering as sometimes your spine needs to move spontaneously as energies are awakened and released.

1 - Step into Awareness

Foundation Breath Meditation
10 minutes

I would recommend you do this twice each day for 3 days before going on to the next meditation and then use it as a preparatory meditation for all future work. If you do nothing else towards your personal development I recommend you do this. It will change everything.

Close your eyes and begin to focus on your breath.

As you exhale, allow yourself to release.

Exhale... Release physical tension.
Exhale... Release judgement, criticism, and analysis.
Exhale... Release all thought.

Continue breathing...

Watch each breath...

Notice how it feels to bring air into your body and to feel your lungs and chest expand.

Breathe... notice the emptying as you exhale.

Allow your lungs to empty completely... and slowly inhale to your full capacity.

Gently exhale completely.

Do this 3 times.

Continue to breathe… find your natural rhythm. Let it be; don't attempt to change it.

Ignore thoughts about 'good' breathing or 'bad' breathing; just accept what is.

As you exhale, let go of these or any other thoughts… breathe away self-judgement and criticism… Release physical tension… Release all thought…

Now, as you inhale, allow your expanding breath to energise you. Let the breath fill you with swirling, sparkling energy….

Watch your internal world as each inhale brings replenishing nourishment into your body. Do this 3 times.

If a thought comes in, breathe it away on your next exhale, and bring your focus back to the breath….

Do you have any thoughts or judgements? Simply notice them… then let them go on the next exhale… breathe them away…. breathe…

Allow the inhale to expand your mind… feel the sense of space there…

Breathe… breathe… breathe…

If a thought comes in, let it go.

Breathe… Allow the inhale to expand consciousness.

1 - Step into Awareness

Breathe… allow the breath to create space.

Another thought?

Catch it… observe it …breathe it out… let it go… then bring your awareness back to the breath.

Breathe… breathe… breathe…

Continue in this manner, noticing and releasing thoughts, remaining in awareness of your breath, allowing your breath to be, and expanding your inner world.

When the time is up (unless you are moving on to another practice) take 3 deep, cleansing and energising breaths. With each breath allow yourself to become more and more conscious of your physical body.

Feel the weight of your body against the chair or the floor. Become aware of the room or the environment you are in.

When you are ready, gently open your eyes.

Use this **foundation breath meditation** to centre and realign yourself before all future work. Your consciousness will learn to recognise it as a sign that you will be doing some transformational work and it will make itself ready.

Body – the Manifest Being

The body is your first connection to the world around you. When you see, hear, touch, taste, and smell your body is perceiving some of the energies that surround you and interpreting them – making sense of the vast assortment of vibration. You interpret your world via this information. As well as the most obvious and immediate objects around you, your senses also retain information you are not consciously aware of.

When you step outside your senses of smell and taste detect the quality of the air – your senses know who just walked past your house and what they had eaten for breakfast. Your ears pick up information about what is happening 10 meters away and even 10 miles away. Your sense of touch tells you whether the air is damp or dry, whether it's hot or cold, and it gives you information about the possible impending weather conditions. When you shake someone's hand or kiss them you are receiving messages about their genetic code. The smell of someone's sweat gives you information about their health and their mood.

These messages are going directly to your unconscious and pre-conscious mind, and your behaviour is modified by this information. You just don't know it. The following meditations on the body are a step towards understanding just how amazing you are and exactly what tools you have at your disposal.

1 - Step into Awareness

These meditations will also bring about changes in the choices you make about how you use your body on a day-to-day basis. Many spiritual practices advise you to sit, walk, eat, drink, or even sleep according to particular rules or dogma. The advice may be useful, but it could also be wrong for you. People may struggle with some of the requirements of their chosen religion or spiritual practice and then criticise themselves for failing or for not being 'spiritual' enough.

There is little point in blindly following instructions without question no matter how much respect you might have for a teacher, guru, spiritual book, or priest. Until behaviour comes from your own truth it will be inconsistent and difficult to retain. If you discover what is correct for your own body by listening to its wisdom, the behaviour will change automatically and you will have a better chance of sustaining the changes.

You may even end up at the same destination (you might not), but you will have arrived from your own experience and internal knowledge. Using these meditations, any new behaviour that you take on, or any old behaviour that falls away, will happen because this is correct and healthy for you not because you have been told that this is how a 'spiritual' person behaves. The following meditations will allow you to look at your everyday choices and learn to notice how these choices affect your well-being.

Body Sensation Meditation
20 minutes

*Close your eyes and centre yourself for a few minutes with the **foundation breath meditation** (p.63).*

Now take your attention deep inside your body. Where does this attention initially find its home? Is it in your heart, your stomach, your head?

Notice where 'you' are... how does it feel in here? What does it look like?

Observe... simply... gently....

Now, slowly begin to move around this inner world that is 'you'...

Explore...

Explore your internal world slowly, all the way from the top of your head to the tips of your toes.

As you move from one area to another, allow yourself to pause and really be present with each part. Notice what is happening there.

What can you see? Are there any colours or shapes? What does it feel like?

As you move to another area, and settle your attention there, notice how the experience alters.

1 - Step into Awareness

Can you observe your internal organs? Can you feel your heart pumping or your intestines gurgling?

What happens as you breathe? Do you notice changes to the internal environment? What do you feel with the exhale... the inhale?

You may notice your mind trailing off. By simply noticing this it will bring you back to awareness.

Take it slowly... allow yourself time to feel... to notice...

What are the sensations? Is it tingling, electrical impulses, heat, or cold?

Do you notice any tension or any tightness? Watch it. What happens when you give it your attention? Don't force it away, simply notice it and breathe...

When the time is up, centre yourself and feel balanced. Let your awareness expand to incorporate your whole body. Use your breath to connect you, and bring your consciousness back to the waking reality.

Take three deep and energising breaths, and, when you are ready, open your eyes.

Do this once or twice each day for 3 days. Notice any changes. Watch without judgement. Explore with love and self-acceptance.

Thought – the Stream of Delusion

There is a common misunderstanding that to meditate is to sit in silence with an empty mind. This is definitely one of the outcomes after years of practice – the more you meditate the clearer and stiller your mind will become. But at first this is impossible. The mind has a job and it is very useful job in most circumstances. It makes connections and looks for meaning. It judges situations using information from the senses, memory, and learned knowledge in order to understand and make sense of experience and to keep you safe from perceived danger. It offers information through the senses, and through the emotions of anger, fear, shame, and happiness etc. which guide you in social interactions and in your environment.

However, when an individual is ready to move beyond the everyday and into a more enlightened way of being, some of these functions can get in the way of the clarity that is necessary for growth. It is impossible at first to stop the mind doing this work so the first step of meditation is to simply become aware of these unconscious processes as they happen.

The following meditation is an exercise in observing the mind. The more you meditate, and the more you watch yourself and pay attention, the stiller your mind will become, and you will occasionally find yourself in the space between thoughts – the gap. At first you may notice your mind chattering away even more than you ever have. It may feel like it's getting worse. However, the loud,

1 - Step into Awareness

random voices in your head have always been there. Perhaps you have never noticed just how loud and random they have been.

==If you have started to meditate and have noticed your mind chattering away you have succeeded.== In the moment of noticing you are in awareness. This is the goal of meditation. In the following practice you will begin to understand just how the mind works – how it picks up on a stimulus and runs away with it; how it takes your attention off on tangents and follows random connections; how it continually plans, judges, worries, and criticises.

*

==With more practice, meditation brings you the ability to choose when to use the tool of thought and when to be in silence.==

*

Thought Awareness Meditation
20 minutes

Sit comfortably and close your eyes. Begin with a few minutes of the **foundation breath meditation** *(p63).*

As you exhale allow all tension in your body to release.

Notice the in-out rhythm of your breath.

Now, hold the image of a blank screen in your mind and wait. A thought will come. As soon as you become aware of the thought, take hold of it and observe it.

How long has it been there? Where did it come from?

From the point that you noticed and stopped it, begin to trace it back. Follow each thought backwards – the images and the words. Follow the trail of digressions until you find the initiating thought.

What inspired it... was it a child's voice or a phone ringing?

When you find the original thought, let it go... breathe it away. Silence... breathe...

Soon you will notice that you are thinking again.... you wake up in the middle of a thought trail.

Slow it down... watch the pictures on the screen. Freeze the image.

1 - Step into Awareness

Now, once again, trace it back; follow the thought line backwards. Don't engage... be aware of diversions... keep going back... find the original thought...

Then let it go... breathe... breathe it away.

You may find that while you are tracing your thoughts back, another thought comes in and you go off on a completely different tangent. Let go of your frustration about this. Your mind is just doing its job. Simply pick up the thought where you caught it this time and trace it back.

Breathe it away in the silence...

As you continue to practice, try to notice the thoughts sooner. You may be able to connect immediately with the very first thought. You may be able to notice the silence for longer. When the time is up, take 3 deep, energising breaths, and open your eyes.

Practice this meditation once or twice each day for 3 days and write your observations in your journal. By the time you have finished the 3 days, you may find that you are continually noticing your thoughts throughout the day. Although this may feel as though your mind is working overtime or that you are going backwards in your development, it is simply a sign that you are becoming even more aware of your mind working. This is good. This is your aim – to be in constant awareness. The three meditations described in this chapter can be used at any time for a continued daily practice.

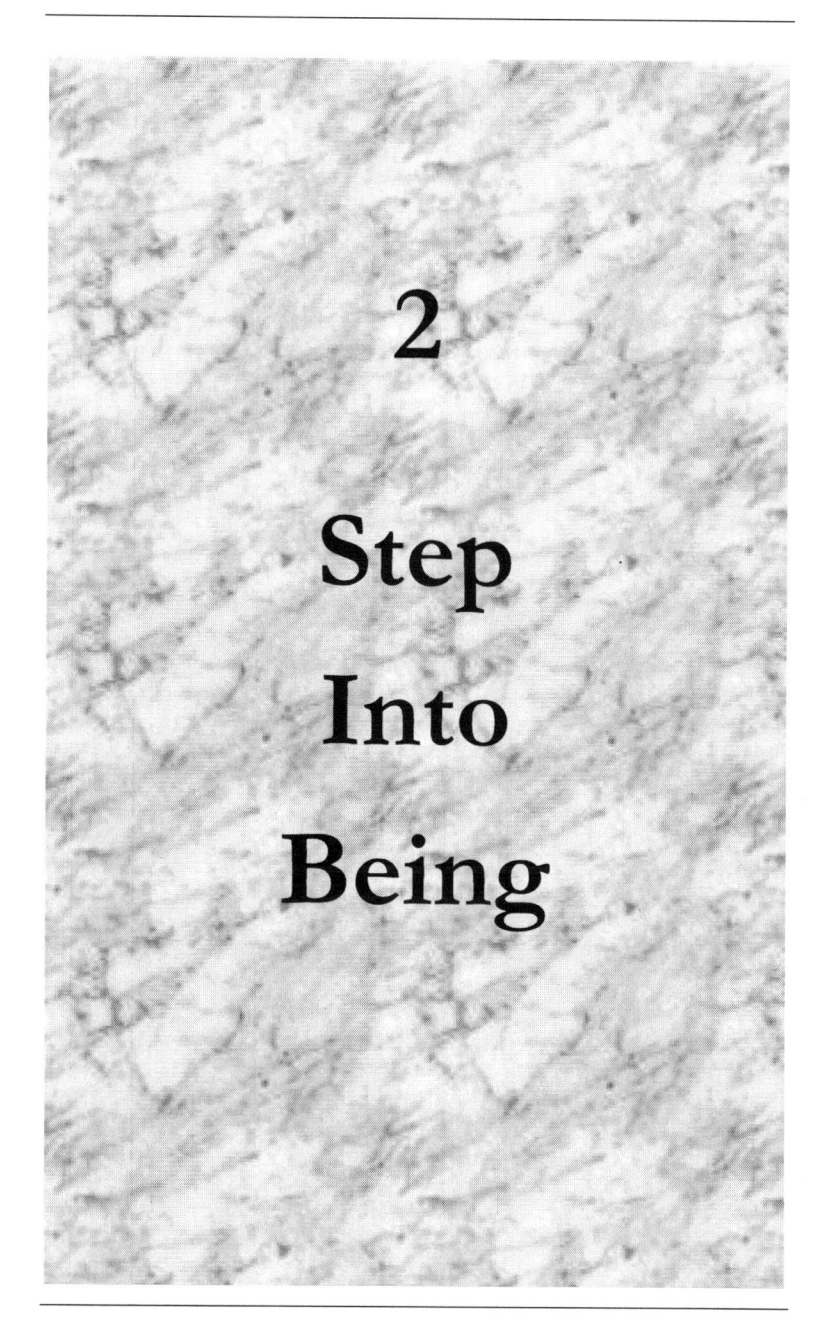

2

Step

Into

Being

2 - Step Into Being

Senses

During the meditations so far, you have been focusing purely on your internal world. The following meditations will now explore the interactions between your internal world and the external environment. The meditations will help you to deeply understand the energetic/vibrational nature of the environment around you. They will also help you to understand how the senses translate this vibration in order to make sense of the external world – giving it shape, form, taste, sound, smell, and colour – and how this translation informs your sense of reality.

We tend to take our senses for granted; the following exercises will encourage you to know the truly amazing skills you have access to. The work will allow you to build on these skills until you become very sensitive to the messages sent from your unconscious. Then, when your unconscious has something important to say, you will know to give it your full attention.

While practising the following exercises, get into the habit of scanning your whole body up and down being careful not to miss any part out. The aim is to experience these meditations as an inquisitive observer – exploring the landscape of the senses. For these meditations you will be asked to prepare items to use. Choose them with care and love, and use them with reverence. Find a beautiful cloth to put them on. Have a sense of ritual, and feel that you are nourishing and loving yourself as you are doing it.

Day 1: Sensation
20 - 30 minutes

Begin this exercise in the morning. Prepare some different objects to explore. I recommend using objects with a variety of textures. Also, choose some objects that you think you will enjoy touching and some things that you would normally avoid — a feather, a wool blanket, hair, baked beans, and frozen peas for example.

*Begin with the **foundation breath meditation** (p.63).*

When you feel connected and centred, begin to focus on the surface of your skin. Experience all the sensations… What is happening? Is there a tingling here, an ache there?

Explore different areas. Spend some time in each one to really gain a sense of it. Try focusing on the sensation of the skin on your knees, then your cheek, and then the crook of your elbow.

Notice your top lip. Can you feel the breath there?

What do your buttocks feel like taking all your weight?

Do the palms of your hands feel different from the backs of your hands? Is there any difference in temperature?

What is the sensation on your feet?

2 - Step Into Being

Can you feel your hairs… on your head, your arms?

When you breathe do your clothes move on your skin? What does this feel like?

Explore the whole experience of flesh. Is it pleasant or unpleasant? You may feel pleasure or even pain when you become aware of the tiny tingling sensations all over your skin. Notice the pleasure and the pain, but try not to get involved with liking or disliking the sensations. Avoid becoming attached to particular sensations. Just explore, examine, and notice.

When you are ready, begin to use your hands to explore the objects you have prepared. Notice the sensation on your fingers and notice your bodily response. Touch different parts of your body with the objects. How does your body respond to the disliked objects? How does your body react to the preferred objects? Notice all your physical reactions.

Simply watch, and try not to respond to feelings of aversion by stopping. Just continue to touch while noticing any sensations. Don't respond to pleasant feelings by allowing them to go on too long. Just notice, without attachment to any one sensation. By not responding you are training yourself to slow down the re-action response.

When you have explored all your objects, put your hands together. What does it feel like to touch yourself? Move your hands around, feel your fingers, your palms… what is the experience? Does the touch create sensations elsewhere in your body? Explore every part of your hands. Move your hands up your arms. Touch your face, your neck… be gentle… be firm… what feels good? What does your body want from your hands? Does it want to be massaged here, caressed there? What happens if you touch your body in an unpleasant way? Explore this.

Spend time allowing your hands to explore your body everywhere you can reach… focus only on the sensation.

Now rest your hands again. Go back to noticing the sensations on the surface of the skin. Just notice; don't react. If you have an itch, just watch it; don't respond. Notice how an itch builds in intensity. Watch how it eventually goes away.

When the time is up, take three breaths to energise and ground yourself.

Spend the rest of the day with this heightened awareness of the sensation of touch. Let touch be the thing you love today. Notice it in every moment. Notice your reactions to accidental touch. How does your body respond? How do you feel holding a hot drink in your hands? What is the sensation of your shoes on your feet? Are they comfortable? Are your socks too tight? How do your feet feel when they are naked? What is the floor like underfoot? Enjoy exploring these sensations. Your skin is the biggest organ of your body. Do you normally listen to its messages? Does anything change when you do? There is no right or wrong. Simply watch your reactions without judgement.

2 - Step Into Being

Day 2: Hearing
20 - 30 minutes

For this exercise, choose some music that you have found inspiring or moving in the past. Avoid music with words or harsh sounds as during the meditation you will have a very receptive consciousness and it is best not to shock yourself when you are in this state. Also, collect some other sounds, like a drum, a bell, or a Tibetan singing bowl for example. Prepare the volume on your music player beforehand so the music begins gently.

*Begin with the **foundation breath meditation** (p.63).*

When you have finished focusing on the breath, bring your awareness to the sensation of hearing.

How does your body react when a sound comes in?

Do you hear only with your ears? Maybe your hairs or your skin also respond to the vibrations.

Can you hear your breath? Can you hear your clothing as it moves against your skin when you breathe?

What other sounds are coming directly from your body? Can you hear your heartbeat? Be with these internal sounds for some time.

Now, gently allow your awareness to move outside your body. What can you hear? Maybe you can hear tiny creaks in the house or the wind or rain outside? You may hear the sound of birds chattering. If you live in a town, can you hear cars or people passing the house? Let the sounds in without engaging with them or reacting to them.

You may notice your mind wandering off with a sound. When you become aware of this, gently bring your focus back. Avoid engaging with any responses. Notice them and let them go.

Allow your awareness to move further away to more distant sounds. Notice your ability to gauge this distance. Do you know whether the sound is moving away or coming closer?

Notice how the sounds inspire images — painting a picture of your unseen environment.

Be open to all sounds. Do they evoke memories from your past? Watch them. Notice the physical sensations and then let the images go.

After a while, begin to make sounds with the instruments you have prepared. Feel the vibrations. Allow them to enter your body. How does it feel? Can you feel the sound in your feet, or in your stomach?

Your lips are extremely sensitive. If you bring an instrument close to your mouth, you might be able to feel the physical sensation of the vibrations.

Explore the different qualities of the instruments near your face. Is your hair sensitive to the vibrations?

2 - Step Into Being

Try making sounds with your mouth... hum, sing, laugh... What happens? What is the sensation?

Now begin to play the recorded music you have prepared. How does the music affect you? Does it feel good? Do you have an emotional response to the music? If so, what sensations does this create?

Does it feel comfortable... or uncomfortable? Notice the bodily response to the sounds. Try to avoid preference with the sensations just notice them all with the same amount of interest.

Do you experience the sound in your ears, your head, or your body? Give yourself permission to feel.

Breathe in the vibrations. Allow the vibration of sound to become a part of you.

When the time is up, bring your awareness back to your environment and feel the weight of your body.

Take three deep, energising, and awakening breaths then open your eyes.

Take this exercise with you for the rest of the day. Allow sound to be the thing you are in love with. Let it be noticed in every moment.

Day 3: Smell
20 - 30 minutes

Prepare different smells that you find pleasant – essential oils, coffee, tea, herbs, chocolate, and flowers, for example. Also, prepare smells which you usually find unpleasant.

*Begin with the **foundation breath meditation** (p.63).*

When you are calm and relaxed, begin to focus on the sensation of smell as you inhale. Can you locate the source of the smell?

Does your mind provide images to accompany the smell? Notice if the smell sensations evoke memories or feelings from the past. Don't engage with these memories on an emotional level. Try not to cling to them. Just watch them and move on remembering that your focus is the sensation of smell.

What happens to your body when you notice a smell? Do you smell with just your nose? Are other parts of your body involved? Continue to work with the random smells that happen to be drifting to you for a while.

Now, begin to bring each prepared item up to your nose. Begin with coffee as this clears your sinuses ready for a new smell. You could use this in-between the other smells if you wish. Take plenty of time with each item to really understand everything that happens to your body.

2 - Step Into Being

Notice how each smell affects you. What do you feel? Where do you feel the sensation? Is it just in your nose, or do you feel it elsewhere in your body?

Do you feel changes in your brain, or in your body? Do different smells have different effects?

How does your body react differently to each smell? Do any of the smells create images, or memories? Do the smells evoke different colours?

Do you notice your gastric juices begin to flow when you smell an item that you would like to taste? Do you notice your stomach? Do the sensations change there? What is the difference when you smell a food item and a non-food item? Which smells do you prefer? Why?

Try one of the unpleasant smells. What do you notice about your reaction? Does it affect your whole body?

Continue to explore in this way noticing the sensations in your body.

When the time is up, focus on your body and the weight of your body against the floor or the chair. Take three deep, energising breaths to bring yourself back to everyday consciousness, and open your eyes.

For the rest of the day focus your attention on the sensation and experience of smell. Let smell be your guide for today, and listen to the information you receive from your body via the world of smell. Love smells for the whole day.

Day 4: Taste
20 - 30 minutes

As you did yesterday, prepare lots of items. This time prepare things that you can eat. Try to include foods that are bitter, salt, sweet, and sour tasting. Also include some natural and some mass-produced food, and some items which you find pleasant and some you find unpleasant.

*Begin with the **foundation breath meditation** (p.63).*

When you are settled and centred, begin your exploration of taste.

Start with what's already there…

What does your tongue taste like? How does it taste inside your mouth? Open your mouth. What does your breath taste like? Can you taste the air? Can you taste the items you have prepared on the air?

Do you taste with just your tongue? Do the sensations spread inside your body? How does your body feel when a new taste enters?

Begin to taste the prepared items… slowly, and with great attention.

What does each taste feel like? Notice the sensations in your body. Do you feel them just in your mouth or in your toes as well?

2 - Step Into Being

Do you notice a colour, thought, or memory attached to a taste? Does it raise any emotions?

How does your body react to each flavour?

Is your body reacting with craving or aversion? Try to watch with interest but not with preference. If your body reacted with aversion, try this taste again... and again...

What is happening to your body? If your body reacted with craving, see what happens when you don't offer this taste again. Does your mind attempt to convince you to take more or does it feel like more of a physical desire?

Continue exploring the tastes in this way until the time is up.

Then focus on the weight of your body. Take your three energising breaths and finish the exercise gently. When you are ready, open your eyes.

For the rest of the day give your attention to taste. Let your consciousness live on your tongue and let taste fill every moment. Notice what happens when you feel hungry or full. What changes occur? How does your body give you this information? When you are not eating can you notice the subtle taste sensations you experience in your mouth as the day progresses? When you do eat, try eating slowly and with full attention – tasting every mouthful and monitoring your response.

Day 5: Sight
20 - 30 minutes

Prepare some items to look at. For example: a computer screen, a book, a feather, some flowers, and a toy from childhood. Include objects with strong and gentle colours. Include: something you dislike and something you like, something from nature and something technological, and something handmade and something mass produced. Find some photos – include pictures of a loved one, a celebrity, and someone you don't like. Also position a mirror in front of you so you can see yourself while you are meditating, but for now cover it with a cloth.

*Begin with the **foundation breath meditation** (p.63) and then bring your internal focus to the back of your eyelids. With your eyes closed, look at the back of your eyelids. What do you actually see there... colours, spirals, sparkles? How does it feel? Explore this area for a while.*

Gently open your eyes... notice what happens... how does this invasion of light affect your sensations? What do you feel? What happens to your body? What does the light feel like? Begin to look around the room. How do your eyes move around? What are they drawn to? How do the images affect your sensations?

Now focus on your chosen items. Look at them one by one. Notice your physical response. Don't engage with the thoughts they inspire. Let the thoughts go, and focus on your sensations. Allow your attention to move up

2 - Step Into Being

and down your body in waves – checking for response and reaction. Don't get involved. Just notice.

What happens to your body when you look at something that appeals to you? What happens when you see something disturbing? What are the sensations?

Let your thoughts go and focus on the sensations. Where do you feel the reaction – in your heart, in your stomach, in your fingers? Continue scanning your whole body for sensations.

Continue this until you have explored all your items except the mirror, leave this until last. When you are ready, remove the cover from the mirror and look at your reflection.

Immediately notice your physical response and sensations. How does your own reflection affect you? What happens when you are faced with yourself? You may notice your mind making judgments; you may notice emotions. Notice but don't engage with the thoughts. Let them go.

Explore your reflection and your reactions for a while. When you have finished, take three long breaths to awaken and energise yourself.

For the rest of the day focus on your sense of vision and the sensations, emotions, and judgments it arouses. Once again, just notice without trying to find meaning and without engaging with the thoughts. Let vision be the thing you love today.

Day 6: The Sixth Sense

As you may have now seen, your senses are vital tools in the development of self awareness. Noticing your reaction to smell, sound, taste, touch, and vision is a huge step towards knowing yourself. As you move on in your journey of growth it is also important to begin to notice your more subtle senses. These senses speak to you via feelings, hunches, signs, subtle sensations and intuition.

As you continue in your meditation practice you will find yourself noticing these subtle experiences more and more. You may even wish to follow the intuitive hunches, they might lead you somewhere. Did you see something out of the corner of your eye? Did you get a sense of something stroking your cheek? Did you feel a tingling in your feet? Did you hear a whisper? Learn to accept any of these subtle messages and to listen to them. None of them are there by accident – they are coming to your awareness for a reason.

As we grow up we are taught to take no notice of these subtle experiences. Perhaps it's time to invite these experiences back?

> *Spend time exploring your environment with your sixth sense (the subtle experience of the vibrations around you) using the palms of your hands, your lips or cheeks, or the hairs on your arms and head. Explore the energetic sensation of different objects without actually touching them. With half closed eyes you might able to see colourful energetic fields around people and things as well.*

2 - Step Into Being

Does the object have a sense of heat or cold, or pushing or sucking?

How does the subtle energy of a flower feel in the space near the palms of your hands?

How does this differ from the energy of a stone?

Does plastic have an energy you can feel? What about wood or metal?

Explore the energy of different crystals. When you have understood the differences in the way each crystal feels, see if you can you identify them with your eyes closed, just by feeling them with your sixth sense. Can you do this with different colours as well?

Play with energy. Can you pass it to someone else? Can you move it around? Can you shape it?

Can you feel or see the energy of another person? How does the sensation of their energy vary around different parts of their body?

Explore the subtle nature of energy at every opportunity, as this will help you to understand the nature of reality and to become more sensitive to your intuitive messages. Attempt to notice these more subtle energies around you all the time. Follow your 'gut' responses and see where they lead. Notice the invisible sensations that whisper past your body, or the vague images that float through your mind and across your vision.

Environment

In the majority of spiritual practice there is much focus on meditation that is practiced while the body is still. There are many stories told about spiritual masters who take themselves off into the wilderness for 40 days and nights living in solitude on mountains or in caves, or sitting under trees for hours on end. It is often suggested that lengthy meditation is the ideal or the only way to reach enlightenment.

But what about those who have full-time jobs, children to look after, or homes to organise? There is something to be valued in solitude and inactivity but these are not essential for enlightenment. Once a regular routine of daily sitting meditation has been established and the consciousness is practiced at remaining in awareness, the practice can be applied throughout the activities of the day. Washing up can be a wonderful experience when experienced in 'now' consciousness.

The following exercises use your normal everyday activities as conscious points of learning and growing. Having explored the senses one by one, you will now be using your body and all the senses as one. Keep the focus on your sensations and work at simply observing – there should be no judgement and no analysis. Do not try to change anything. Trust that the natural healing capacity of your body will make any necessary changes without your conscious interference. By doing this you will create change that is perfect for you, rather than change that you or someone else thinks is correct.

Walking Meditation
1 day

Go for a walk, or use your daily walk to work/school/shop. While you are walking, take your attention inside your body...

Be present.

Notice your breath and begin to ask yourself questions.

What is happening as you walk?

Does the breath change at all?

Are your arms swinging? Do they swing freely? Are they symmetrical or asymmetrical?

Do you notice any tension, or any stiffness?

What do you notice about the ground? Is it hard or soft? How does this affect your body or your style of walking?

Carry your awareness deeper into your body. Can you feel your heart beating?

Notice your movements. How does your left foot fall on the ground? Does it fall in the same way as your right foot?

Can you hear anything? How does your body change when a sound comes in? How does the sound of birdsong affect you? What happens when you hear a car rush past unexpectedly?

Notice how you feel when you're walking to work. Do you feel differently if you are walking to a friend's house, or to the shops, or to the park?

Be in the now; be present in the moment, and use all of your senses to the full.

Notice everything — your breath, the smells, the tastes, the sounds, and the sensations in your body.

No judgement or analysis.

At some points, stop — just there in the moment — hold yourself in freeze frame.

Wait… watch…

What do you feel? Do you have any tension? Are you heavier on one side than the other? Where is your centre of gravity?

At some point you will begin to move again. Do you know what the impetus for movement was? Continue to walk and notice.

Do this meditation consciously for the whole day, and in future as often as you remember. Soon, whenever you are walking, the constant awareness of your body and its responses will become second nature.

2 - Step Into Being

Eating Meditation
1 day

All food has a herbal/medicinal property in that it has an effect of change on your body. It is easy to understand the effects of things that have a gross and immediate effect, coffee or alcohol for example, but what about food and drinks that have a more subtle effect? Use this meditation to bring awareness to your eating patterns and the effects that your food choices, and the way you eat your chosen food, have on your body.

When you sit down with your meal, bring yourself to the present moment and notice how the food looks. Notice how you feel about the particular food on your plate.

Now carefully choose a morsel to taste, place it in your mouth and begin to chew it really slowly. Chew for much longer than you normally would before you swallow. Be totally present to this morsel in your mouth. Spend time with this meal. Be present. Notice what happens and notice the sensations.

As you go through your day notice how different situations affect you. Notice your habits around food.

What happens when a food is cooked? It not only tastes different, but does it affect you in a different way? Does one type of food make you salivate more than another? Does any food make you sweat? Does it change the beating of your heart? Compare the experience of eating a raw organic carrot to the experience of eating some crisps or sweets. What do you notice? How does coffee and tea affect you compared to water? How does your body respond? Forget about information you have been given previously and notice what the food is actually doing to your body – you might be surprised.

What does hunger really feel like? How do you know if you are hungry? What are the sensations?

What happens if you eat too much? How do you know when you have had enough? What is the sensation? Can you stop eating then?

Some foods may affect your body straight away. Some may take 20 minutes, an hour, or even a day to have an effect. Keep your awareness on your body to notice these changes and subtle sensations. Particularly notice your skin, your digestive tract, your breathing, your mucus membranes, and your heartbeat. Receive the information and notice your reactions.

For the whole day, and as often as you remember after that, take your time while you eat and notice your responses. As you become aware of your responses, try not to judge yourself and don't change anything consciously. If things are unhelpful for you, they will fall away naturally. Trust your deeper consciousness to do the work for you. If you become aware of your sensations and reactions, your body will look after itself and work towards its own self-healing. It will be free to make useful choices rather than be a slave to craving.

Outer World Meditation
2 or 3 days

Having worked with food and drink, it is now time to look at the more subtle ways you ingest your environment. You are affected by everything – the air around you, sunlight, darkness, other people's energies, traffic fumes, emissions from unnatural lighting, computer screens, Wi-Fi technology, TV, etc.

For the next two or three days, aim to be completely present with everything you do: brushing your teeth, washing up, exercising, playing sport, getting dressed, being at work, holding a baby, watching TV, etc.

While you are in awareness, listen to your body. Let it communicate with you; let it give you information about your environment.

Take yourself to places you visit in a normal day, but also explore new environments as well. Feel the difference between standing on the pavement at the side of a busy road and standing in a quiet place in nature.

Explore your reactions to each room in your home and your place of work. Visit a friend or go to a library, the cinema, a café, a restaurant, a yoga class, or a nightclub. Explore your sensations and your reactions in as many different locations as you can find.

As always, don't get involved with any emotional responses, old stories, or meanings that your mind creates.

Work hard at staying with the physical sensations of the now. Just notice them. There's no need to name or analyse them. Notice and explore your sensations in each moment.

The work of exploring yourself in these ways will lead you to deep self-knowledge. All of these meditations serve the same purpose – self observation and being present to the moment.

Regular practice is useful to help you develop the new habit of stopping in the moment and becoming aware of thoughts, feelings, fantasies, or frustrations, in whatever you are doing. You can then choose to either let these thoughts go or act on them. This process will help you to notice your physiological and emotional reactions and responses to your environment without mindlessly re-acting. If you do find yourself reacting, because you didn't catch yourself in the first moment of response, you can use this as an opportunity to learn. As soon as you remember, become present and then watch what happens to your body during a re-action.

This may also help you to understand exactly how your body is creating your experience in every moment. How YOU are responsible for your experience of the world around you.

*

Becoming conscious of exactly what you have previously been doing unconsciously is a step towards taking responsibility for the creation of your own experience.

*

Other People

Having asked you to explore your responses to objects of the outside world, the next step is to become aware of your responses to other people. Little-you motivates your behaviour in many ways. The work here is to observe yourself when you are in communication and interaction. Notice your body language and your facial expressions and, very importantly, be aware of your sensations. Your responses give you important information about yourself. Following are some awareness exercises for use during interaction. During the practice, aim to be particularly aware of the level of anxiety you have. This is a very clear indicator of your survival mechanism in action. As little-you feels more or less threatened your levels of anxiety will rise and fall accordingly.

Some of the signs of anxiety are:

- ❖ Tightness across the chest.
- ❖ Shallow and fast breathing.
- ❖ Facial flushing or blanching.
- ❖ Foggy brain.
- ❖ Sweaty palms.
- ❖ Butterflies in the stomach.
- ❖ Feelings of wanting to disappear, run away, or hide.
- ❖ Inability or reluctance to speak.
- ❖ Sudden rushes of anger or fear.
- ❖ Palpitations.
- ❖ Shaking.
- ❖ Fast eye movements.

If you feel any of these sensations (and you are not in any immediate physical danger) it is a reminder that you have been triggered by something and you are now experiencing feelings that are directly related to a past memory or trauma. You may have a strong impulse to react. You might become angry or defensive, or feel shy and quiet. You may want to run away. When you experience powerful emotions it is easy to imagine that they are caused someone else's actions in the here-and-now. In this case you might leap to blame the other, you might attempt to punish them in order to 'hurt them back', or you might even allow yourself to become a victim.

At first, simply watch your reactions during these exercises. But, as this noticing becomes second nature you can take the next step of reminding yourself that your current feelings are <u>based on something that happened in the past</u>. The present experience will have some similar details to this past event. If you consistently remember this, over time the reactive responses will begin to fall away. With a few conscious deep breaths, some vigorous activity (5 star jumps should do it), and some self-love, the anxiety will fall away too.

In moments of high anxiety this process is easier said than done, and it can be very difficult to even take one conscious breath never mind breathe the reactions away. This is where the regular daily meditation practice comes in handy. The meditations give you new habits of non-reaction and eventually the breathing away of unhelpful reactivity will become second nature, even in moments of high anxiety. I have given some examples below, but there are many more experiences that you could explore.

Re-action in Conversation

You find yourself in a conversation. Catch yourself in the present moment and take some time to centre yourself by breathing consciously.

Now take your attention back to the conversation while remaining in awareness. What do you feel?

Notice what motivates you to speak, or smile, or keep quiet.

Do you want to be liked? Are you trying to show that you are knowledgeable?

Do you feel a real need to get your words out or to be heard? Are you feeling impatient?

Is there any anxiety?

Notice your non-verbal communication. What is your body saying?

When you have watched your normal behaviour for a while, play around with different ways of behaving.

When you have an urge to speak notice it but hold the moment...

Feel... what is motivating me to say this?

What happens when you miss that vital opportunity to get your point across? What do you notice in your body? What does 'little-you' feel?

If someone says something you disagree with, what happens if you simply smile and nod rather than jump in with your argument?

What happens to you and your body if you say something that you wouldn't normally say out-loud? For example, 'I'm feeling bored of this conversation' or 'I'm feeling irritated by what you just said'.

If you are normally quiet, allow yourself to be more talkative, think of some things to say, interrupt someone. How does this feel?

What happens to you if people seem annoyed? What feelings and sensations do you have?

At all times be attentive to your feelings, sensations, motivations, movements, and facial expressions. Be in the moment. Whatever you are doing there is always an opportunity to observe.

Re-action in Conflict

In a conflict or argument the first step of awareness is to simply notice your default behaviour.

Someone is challenging you. Do you feel defensive or perhaps disappointed?

Someone has not behaved in the way you expected or wanted. What do you do?

What are your feelings and sensations? What motivates you? Is it self-righteousness?

Are you motivated to punish the other person or blame them?

Be very aware of the sensations in your body. Do you feel like running away, or attacking, or do you feel stuck? Is your chest tightening? Do you feel a wave of excitement, fear, or anxiety?

Simply notice your normal response with love, no self judgment.

Having become aware of your habitual responses, play with some new ones. Try out different possibilities.

❖ *Next time you are in a conflict situation and are ready to react, simply stop. Notice your sensations and take a breath. Just as you have practiced in the meditations, notice what is happening but don't act on any of your feelings. Take a breath, and smile to yourself. What happens?*

- *Try being in the moment, rather than focusing on past events, and notice what is happening in your body. For example: 'My stomach is in knots', 'my head is spinning', 'I feel out of breath'. What happens to you when you share this?*

- *When you speak, instead of saying what you think the other person did wrong or what you want them to do, say what you feel. For example: 'I feel sad/anxious/scared because this situation is different to what I expected'.*

- *Notice what happens when you take responsibility for your reactions?*

If you begin to recognise your reactions as your own creation then it becomes easier to understand that the reactions of others are their creation too. It helps to keep these separate and to not take other people's reactions and projections personally.

Re-action during Sexual Connection

During a sexual encounter, begin by noticing your habitual responses. How do you feel about the person/people you are with? Do you connect deeply with them or do you feel distant or distracted?

How do you respond to touch?

What thoughts or fantasies are you having? What happens if you stop thinking and focus on the present moment?

Do you feel safe? Is there any anxiety?

What happens if a person you are with suggests or tries something you are not in the mood for or you don't feel comfortable with? Can you say no? Do you go ahead anyway? Do you feel shame, sadness, frustration, or boredom?

What kind of sounds do you make? Are they genuine? Are you consciously being louder or quieter?

What happens if a person you are with does not want to do what you want them to? What happens if they behave differently to how you expect or want?

How does your body move? Is this movement natural, or are you exaggerating the movements or making them smaller?

Do you use words?

What are you seeing, smelling, tasting, hearing and feeling? Do you have any judgements?

Now you have noticed your usual response to a sexual connection, next time play around with different possibilities. You could explain what you are doing to the person/people you are with if you felt it appropriate.

- ❖ *Refrain from thought or fantasy and focus only on the physical sensations. How does this change your experience?*

- ❖ *What happens if you stop moving? Be still in the moment and breathe. What are the sensations and feelings?*

- ❖ *What happens if you allow your body to move freely or without your conscious interference?*

- ❖ *Try focusing only on the breath. Breathe deeper. Do you notice anything?*

- ❖ *Experiment with your voice. How do the sounds you are making change your experience? What happens in your body if you make no sound?*

- ❖ *Feel the difference that happens when you speak or don't speak. Say out loud what you need and what you want; say what you don't want. How does this feel? What happens if you remain silent?*

2 - Step Into Being

- ❖ *Try moving in different ways. How does this change your experience?*

- ❖ *Try something you've have been afraid to try. Do you notice anxiety?*

- ❖ *What happens if you totally surrender to the moment, give yourself completely? No thought, just breathing and sensation. Do you feel safe or liberated?*

- ❖ *Keep your eyes closed. Do you feel connected? Try looking deeply into a person's eyes, holding the gaze. Does anything change?*

Continue this work until you begin to really understand what is right for you and good for you. Allow your body to release unnecessary behaviours naturally.

By now, you should have gained some insights into your interaction with things and people outside of yourself. If you can continue to hold this inner awareness at all times you will begin to feel free from the limitations of 'little-you' fears and needs. You will be able to really take responsibility, not only for your perceptions and therefore your creations in the environment around you, but for your re-actions to situations and interactions. If you continue daily with this practice, your calm, balanced, and happy state will remain, even in very challenging situations. You will have taken responsibility for yourself and your creations.

3

Step
Into
Responsibility

3 - Step Into Responsibility

Release Fear from the Mind

As you work through these exercises and become aware, you will begin to notice your self-critical or negative voice more and more. For example, you might hear thoughts like: 'that's a stupid thing to think/say/do', or 'you can't wear that, what will people think', or 'keep quiet', etc. As I have already described, these thoughts come from the part of you that learned in early childhood how to be an acceptable, and therefore 'safe', human being. Humans have a powerful survival instinct. We are, essentially, pack animals and we rely on our group for protection, so our survival mechanism tells us to 'fit in'. In close communities or 'tribes' it is very important that humans follow the rules of their group. If they don't they may be rejected, and this could be life threatening.

From the minute we are born we are processing information about the rules of our 'tribe'. Nowadays, this 'tribe' will be the situation or family that we are born into and the environments we spend a lot of our time in, such as schools. In contemporary culture, even though non-conforming is not necessarily life threatening (although sadly in some cases it is), we still have the same survival mechanism. As we develop, we very quickly learn to behave in ways that are acceptable and that draw approval from the carers and peers. Every tribe offers different experiences, values, and beliefs. It is these, together with the 'rules' and punishments, that create deep pathways in the brain and that will shape our adult behaviour and our perception of the world.

For example, if a family values education and intellect they will praise a child for working hard. The child experiences approval and learns to exaggerate this behaviour. They will unconsciously repeat sentences to themselves like: 'I must do my best', or 'I must be perfect'. Or if they struggle with education, the sentences might be: 'I'm not good enough', or 'I'm stupid'. Another family might find intellect threatening and show disapproval if the child does well in education. This child will learn to hide, or even lose, their intellectual abilities and will repeat sentences like: 'I shouldn't be a show-off', or 'reading is a waste of time'.

Another common trauma for children, particularly those below the age of four years, is when a younger sibling enters the household. The parents' (and particularly the mother's) attention is often suddenly directed onto another child. This can feel like a threat to life. The daily repeated experience of this can lead to internal beliefs about not being loved, being rejected, being less important, and therefore being in danger. These children learn to either stifle or exaggerate their natural urges of asking for love and attention.

There are extreme circumstances, such as repeated bullying at school, or verbal, physical, or sexual abuse, that will make this process even more debilitating. The results of disapproval here can cause physical pain and massive emotional trauma. Therefore these children may stifle all their natural behaviour in favour of any behaviour that the abuser asks of them, hoping that this will make a difference.

3 - Step Into Responsibility

These unconscious thoughts and behaviours are necessary in childhood as they enable the child to adjust according to expectations. As you grow and change, and move in different circles, these rules are no longer needed, but the protective inner voice remains the same. It doesn't grow with you. The little-you residing inside the adult will continue to follow the same rules and to believe the same thoughts. No matter how much the environment changes, little-you still experiences the world as if it were the same. It also projects the faces of its remembered tribe onto anyone it comes into contact with and therefore presumes their actions will be the same. Little-you brings your past stories into the present.

Little-you will put unnecessary emphasis on stimuli making certain information overly exaggerated. You will <u>always</u> notice events that seem to 'prove' your false beliefs, but you will <u>never</u> notice events that suggest the opposite. In some cases this can seem absurd – even to yourself. For example: in a relationship with someone, you may continue to insist that they don't love you no matter how much they try to prove otherwise.

Fear held in the mind changes your behaviour and shapes your perception and focus. As you have experienced (in the previous meditations that focused on the senses) the outer world is nothing more than energy and vibration from which millions of different possibilities can be perceived. You will choose your focus according to what you believe, and <u>everything else disappears!</u> This is what shapes the reality of your personal universe. Unconscious fear runs the show!

Clear Old Belief Patterns

It is important that you observe these thoughts, but it is equally important that you don't engage with them or react to them, as described in the meditation practices. Because:

*

None of these thoughts are true!

*

Alongside your meditations, you can use the following technique. It will enable you to begin to let go of the unhelpful and fearful thoughts. Bearing in mind that these habits have been with you for the majority of your life, you may need to persevere with this. Do this with patience and gentleness. Remember you are dealing with a 'child' who may feel sacred, lost, and alone.

Carry a small notepad and pen with you at all times. Every time you observe an unhelpful thought, write it down.

It can help to remember the specific childhood situation that this feeling or thought reminds you of as this puts the experience into the past where it belongs, although the practice will still work without this.

Thank little-you for looking after you.

Remind yourself that these are re-actions arising from past experience and therefore not relevant to the here and now.

3 - Step Into Responsibility

For a while, it may feel like the thoughts are spiralling out of control, and you will find yourself writing the same things over and over again. Depending on your childhood environment, you may notice a theme emerging, for example: 'I'm not good enough', 'I don't have enough time', 'I don't have enough money', 'I'll never succeed at this', or 'I am going to be ill'. Any unhelpful thoughts about the unhelpful thoughts need to be written down as well – for example: "I'm so stupid for thinking all these things about myself". Allow yourself to simply notice try not to engage with the thoughts.

Another reason these old beliefs remain is because little-you has never been able to speak them out loud, or has never really been heard. By making these thoughts and fears conscious, and writing them down, you are showing little-you that s/he has been heard. As you write the thoughts down, give little-you some gratitude. Say thank you to this old/child part of you and smile at its love for you, but also remind it that things have changed now. Recall some recent memories where it has been ok to have been imperfect or to have made a mistake.

Having written the thoughts down, the information has been brought to awareness and is now in the hands of a grown-up (you) who can love little-you and take charge of the situation. The distance that you create between you and the thoughts will enable you to disengage from them and to simply observe. You will then be able to run your show from a more calm and conscious place.

A New Internal Story – Angelic Love

You may notice, when you look into the deeper meaning, that your repeated thoughts reduce down to one simple fear. It will be something that sounds like: 'I won't be loved', or 'I'm not good enough'.

The remedy for this is <u>self-love</u>. As an adult, <u>you</u> and <u>only you</u> can instil in yourself a deep feeling of safety, acceptance, and eternal unconditional love.

*

You will never find eternal unconditional love outside of yourself.

*

If you rely on others to create these feelings in you, you will eventually be disappointed. Other people have their own life, their own will, and their own conditions. They leave, they have their own needs to attend to, they argue with you, or they may even die. To be truly happy and fearless, you need to find an inner self-love. This leaves you free to love yourself and others without neediness.

> *Every morning and evening visualise the unhelpful thoughts that you've written down drifting away one by one.*
>
> *Tell little-you that s/he is safe now and that all the fears are unnecessary. Visualise giving your little-self a huge reassuring hug and open to a feeling of love.*

3 - Step Into Responsibility

While little-you is held safely, visualise your grown-up self falling backwards into huge, soft, unconditional, and angelic loving arms...

They hold both of you with absolute unconditional love. The angelic being looks deeply into your eyes and smiles down at you.

Close your eyes and smile – knowing you are safe.

Breathe the smile through your whole body.

Believe that this angelic being and its love for you is real.

Allow yourself to feel completely and utterly safe and loved. Exaggerate this feeling and inhale it.

Use this angelic being as a 'hug and love' mechanism.

The more you use it, the more effective it will become.

It is very important that you FEEL, rather than just think this image. It is the FEELINGS that you create in your body that will make the changes. If you do this regularly for a number of weeks, the new habitual thinking and feeling will create different pathways in your brain, giving you a new story of YOU to live your life by. The previous meditations, this exercise, and the rituals and practices coming up will help you to compound these new habits and beliefs about yourself.

Release Fear from the Body

Another way that little-you attempts to protect is via your body. Your feelings and sensations are messages from the unconscious potentially giving you useful information about the state of your body and your immediate experience. But, for most, these messages are based on fear that comes from past experience rather than the present reality, and therefore the information is incorrect.

If they are not brought to consciousness, past feelings, sensations, and reactions become locked in the body. For example, if a child was frightened to speak it may result in tension around the neck and throat area as they continually hold back their words. Another example happens with physical trauma to the body. During an accident the body braces ready for impact. This involuntary movement can then repeat imperceptibly, for years, causing long-term pain. Even though the original source of fear is in the past, when the patterns are laid down in moments of trauma they will continue to repeat until they have been brought to consciousness and then released.

There are many alternative practitioners that surmise that certain emotional difficulties can be diagnosed from specific illnesses or physical ailments. Some that I have heard so far are: 'if your kidneys fail it's because you lost something and you haven't dealt with the grief', 'people overeat because they feel they weren't loved', 'someone who pushes their chest forward is angry'. I agree with the premise that emotional traumas are held in the body, but, in my experience, not everyone holds their traumas in the

3 - Step Into Responsibility

same way. These global interpretations tend to limit the healing process, as people believe that once they have found a reason for their illness or ailment their emotional traumas will go away. But in the same way the fearful thoughts need to be heard, these somatic memories in the body also need the space to express themselves. Your meditation practice will help with this as the awareness will lead to a release of unhelpful tensions. However, it is also useful to really 'get under your skin' and work these through in a focused way.

The following exercises will help you to connect with the tensions, in your face and then in your body, that you live with on a daily basis. By asking questions of your body, you may be able to find the root cause. When feelings, fears, and memories are acknowledged, heard, and fully expressed they have no need to remain. The first step is to discover precisely how and where your body holds these tensions. The following exercises will enable you to do this.

Facial Tension Meditation
20 – 30 minutes

There are thousands of tiny muscles in your face. Over years of habitual expression they become fixed in certain places causing wrinkles and lines and sometimes causing pain. Our inner world has influenced the muscles in our face and body, defining our appearance and posture. Unconsciously, when we communicate with people, we read their facial lines, postures, and bodily tensions, and we glean incredible amounts of information about them. People are also doing the same with us. For example, lines around the eyes might suggest a lot of smiling or laughing and people will probably feel more drawn to you. On the other hand if you have vertical lines on your top lip and above your nose people will unconsciously read you as angry, impatient, or frustrated. The following meditation will bring awareness of your own habitual facial tension.

Begin with the **foundation breath meditation** *(p.63).*

When you are ready, bring your awareness to your face. Notice what is happening there. Notice the tensions. Are your teeth clenching? Notice the tiny muscles in your top lip.

Become conscious of the muscles around your eyes, your forehead, your jaw, and your neck. Don't change anything; just notice.

Now, begin to allow the tensions to grow, allow the movements go to the extreme. For example, if you feel a

3 - Step Into Responsibility

slight tension in your brow, let it exaggerate, and explore the extreme of the movement. It might pull your eyebrows together, closer and closer, until it engages even more muscles in your face. It might raise your eyebrows.

When you arrive at the absolute extreme, stop, hold it, and notice what you are feeling. Notice any other sensations or emotions that are created in your body from this tension.

At this point in the exercise, you may come across a memory, or a few memories, associated with this feeling. Just watch. Then slowly allow the tension to be released.

Find all the areas of tension in your face and follow the same process.

Take your time. What can you discover about yourself?

When you have finished, you may need to stretch and wriggle your face around. You might find that your muscles are more relaxed than they were before. Take three deep, energising breaths and allow yourself to come back to everyday consciousness.

For the rest of the day take opportunities to stop and notice your face. No judgement. Don't attempt to change things consciously. If you force your tensions away you are only pushing the energy deeper again. After doing this exercise, you will notice the tiny tensions in your face more and more. Then the tensions, like the thoughts in the previous exercise, will naturally fall away.

Body Tension Meditation
20 - 30 minutes

Just like your face, your body holds tensions due to repression of emotion or repeated traumatic experiences. Use the following exercise to help bring these to your awareness.

Begin this exercise in a standing position.

Feel your feet firmly on the floor. Look around the room and check for obstacles. When you are ready, begin to focus on your breath and partially close your eyes.

Centre yourself with the **foundation breath meditation** *(p.63), and then allow your attention to be drawn towards an area of tension in your body.*

At first, just notice the tension. Be careful not to lose it. Sometimes the tensions just disappear when you notice them — especially if you have previously practiced 'releasing' exercises in yoga classes for example.

However, for the purposes of this exercise, you need to allow the tension to remain and then hold it in your awareness.

What is happening? Explore it just as it is. Is it in the shoulder, back, or stomach? Hold your attention there and watch. Notice if you have feelings or memories associated with it.

3 - Step Into Responsibility

Now allow the tension to grow and exaggerate. If it is in your shoulder, for example, see where it wants to go. It might rise to your ear or pull forward. Let the movement go to the extreme. Let the body lead. There is no right or wrong movement. Let it be authentic. Allow the tension to grow, and notice as more areas of your body get drawn into the movement. You may find this physically painful, but try to hold the extreme positions for as long as you can.

Notice the sensations. Notice the emotions. What is happening? Are there memories? If so, watch them pass over your mind screen.

You may find some words or images arising. It may be useful to say these out loud.

Notice your body shape. Do you remind yourself of anything? What do you feel?

When you have fully explored a particular tension in your body, and allowed its extreme, begin to release it. You may prefer to let your tension go explosively or slowly. Follow your body's lead.

Try another area of tension. Follow the same process. Give yourself time to deeply explore. Follow all the areas of tension that you find.

When you have finished, give yourself a good shake to aid the release. You may feel lighter and freer. For the rest of the day, continue to be aware of the tensions that come and go as you move around your environment.

Offer your Body New Possibilities

While you have been watching your body's responses during the previous meditations, your role has been passive – you have been simply observing. During this self-observation you will have experienced some of your old traumas releasing and some of your behaviour changing. But having let go of these old limitations, what next? Sometimes your growth into divinity can be blocked further. You can only grow as far as your imagination will allow. If your past has meant that even your imagination is limited then it is helpful to offer yourself new options.

As you may have discovered, your body has previously been limited by past behaviour patterns. However, it is possible to expand your physical experience beyond your previous limitations. The following exercises are designed to bring new alternatives to old patterns of thinking and behaving. They will create new neural pathways and new opportunities for movement, which in turn will give you more choice about the reality that you create.

Like all animals, there are certain movements and postures which reflect our thoughts and feelings. We smile when we are happy or in agreement for example. However, it can also work the other way around. We can use these movements to actually create real emotions within us. Some movements trick the brain into releasing endorphins – 'happy hormones'. The smile meditation below is very useful, particularly when you find yourself stuck in repeated unhelpful thought patterns or in a state of anxiety.

3 - Step Into Responsibility

Smile Meditation
20 – 30 minutes

The true inner smile (rather than a superficial smile) brings an authentic feeling of love and safety into the body. Before you begin, take a moment to notice how you feel right now.

> *Use the **foundation breath meditation** (p.63).*
>
> *When you are feeling centred and clear, bring your attention to your face. Scan your face, head and neck for sensations. Now, keeping the mouth closed, consciously allow the corners of your mouth to rise slightly into a smile.*
>
> *If you don't notice any changes, make the smile bigger. Involve your eyes and your cheeks. You may feel a rush of sensation in your heart or stomach, or across your chest. You may feel a release of tension. You may feel an urge to inhale deeply.*
>
> *Notice the effect this has on your mood. What do you feel? Where does the feeling come in your body? Let this feeling radiate through your whole body. Enjoy it. When the time is up, take three energising breaths, and open your eyes.*

Realise that this happy feeling came from an internal source. Know that you can choose to feel this any time. Take a moment to assess your mood and emotional state as you did at the beginning of this meditation and notice if there is a difference.

Postures Meditation
20 – 30 minutes

The posture is a physical reflection of one's past experience. When the body is put through any kind of trauma it not only maintains the physical memory in the form of tissue scarring, but it can also extend the damage via tensions in the muscles – caused by holding the body in a particular way after an injury.

The posture is also affected by emotional experiences. For example if a child is constantly praised, and therefore feels good about them-self, they may hold their head up high when they walk. On the other hand, if they are constantly told-off and told they are 'bad' or 'wrong' it can eventually manifest in the body as hunched shoulders, for example.

These patterns develop over many years. They can be changed. But they must be changed on all levels. If you simply try to hold your head up, or your back straight, against your habitual impulse, your body will go back to its regular patterns once you stop thinking about it.

This meditation helps you to explore all the feelings and sensations that are created due to certain postures. It asks you to explore postures that you may not have experienced before. By offering your body new possibilities, and by reviewing old ones, you are extending the options that your body has to choose from during your everyday life and you may find that your posture changes naturally. Try out each position for a minute or two, and notice the different feelings and sensations that are raised as you shift from one to another.

3 - Step Into Responsibility

*Begin with the **foundation breath meditation** then when you feel calm and centered do the following:*

- *Sit upright*
- *Sit hunched*
- *Sit relaxed with arms and legs open*
- *Sit with your arms and legs closed*
- *Stand up and look upwards while you open your arms and hands*
- *Stand tall*
- *Stand small*
- *Hold your head up straight with a smile*
- *Drop your head forward*
- *Drop your head to one side*
- *Fold arms*
- *Hold arms out to the side*
- *Hold arms behind*
- *Put your hands on your hips*
- *Push the chest out*
- *Pull the chest in*
- *Sit in a chair and take up as much space as possible*
- *Sit in a chair and take up as little space as possible*
- *Stand with your shoulders raised slightly*
- *Stand with your shoulders raised, a concave chest, and your head dropped forward*
- *Experiment with other postures*

Having done this meditation your mind will be alert to the different postures you hold and the feelings these raise as you move around your everyday life. For the next few days remain in awareness of your posture and notice which postures are habitual for you. When you next have space to

127

enter your inner world, meditate on the personal habitual postures you have discovered and learn about the feelings they are creating for you, just like you did with the above body postures. However, this time, hold your personal habitual postures for 5 minutes or more and really connect-in with the feelings these evoke. Also notice the work that it takes to hold these postures all the time. You may even have memories return to you as you hold these positions.

Take time to write about your experiences and nurture little-you as you go through this process. Always remember, no self judgement, and no conscious alterations to your posture. If it is wrong for you it will fall away naturally as you continue your meditation practice.

3 - Step Into Responsibility

Authentic Movement Meditation
20 – 30 minutes

Conscious dancing is an extremely powerful process. It offers you a way to release, to heal, and to connect with your divine source. So be prepared for a profound experience! Using the body as a means to shift into a deeper consciousness is a practice as old as humankind. Dance can be a sacred and life-changing activity. In many cultures, spontaneous movement is used as a way to connect with the deeper self, or, as is sometimes understood, to connect with gods, spirits, or animal and plant powers.

During this practice try to develop trust that your body knows exactly what it needs to do. You do not need to direct the movement in any way. Authentic dance/movement is a perfect way to vibrate and move your emotional, physical, and spiritual energy. It will restore your body to its natural order. You may uncover blocked memories as you are moving authentically, and the dance will help you to work towards integrating and healing the emotional pains and patterns that may have been created by these.

Do this meditation in silence a few times. You may also wish to try it with music playing. The music may take you to places that you were unable to explore without it. However, any music you choose will influence your experience, so choose it wisely. I find it best to use music that doesn't have words as the words can direct, or limit, the process too much.

Stand in a large open space. Allow your eyelids to soften and partially close (maintaining a blurry awareness of your surroundings in order to avoid collisions while still maintaining a meditative state).

*Begin with the **foundation breath meditation** (p.63) to centre yourself and make yourself ready.*

As the breath is flowing, begin to enter a state of bodily awareness. As you exhale, let go of any thoughts. As you inhale, feel energised by the breath.

Notice how your breath affects your body; notice how your breath moves through you; notice how it moves you.

As you inhale, watch your body expand with the breath; as you exhale, watch your body empty and contract.

Release into the breath until you find yourself relaxing. Begin gently and subtly moving in rhythm with the breath.

Suggest to your body that it is free to express itself and that you won't interrupt. Be with the breath for a while, holding this idea in your mind.

Now allow your body to have the reins. Have the sense that your body is taking control. Create a sense of following rather than leading, and simply watch and wait.

3 - Step Into Responsibility

As you watch, tiny movements begin to emerge. Work only on allowing the movements to grow. Watch as your arms join in with the movements. Watch as your back and hips give way to the breath. Observe your body for any sensations or impulses to move.

Allow any tiny movement impulses to gently expand until they become full body movements.

Take these movements to the extreme. Follow their lead like you did with the tension exercise.

If you feel like making a sound, allow this too.

Let this process continue until your body is leading you through a series of movements. Don't censor and don't stop anything.

Allow any shaking, vibration, sound, dance, memory, or vision. Let them come. Breathe into them and allow them to expand and grow. See where they take you.

Explore your experience for a while. Follow your movement impulses with interest and curiosity.

They may lead you down to the floor or into a corner. You may need to curl up into a ball or leap around the room. Do not question; just flow with the impulses. Remain authentic.

If you notice yourself thinking or attempting to control the movements, return to the breath focus.

As the process goes on, you will find yourself moving deeper and deeper into yourself. The more you let go and trust, the more you will learn.

When you have been moving for at least 20 minutes and you feel like you have reached the end of this particular work, begin to slow down and return to focusing on your breath. Sit down on the floor and bring your awareness back to the here and now.

Recall your experience, write it down, and/or draw pictures.

The more you use authentic movement, the more profoundly healing it will become for you. You can also use this practice to ask your body/inner wisdom specific questions such as: 'why am I in a bad mood today?', 'what shall I do about this relationship?', 'what steps shall I take to heal this illness?', or even 'where did I put my keys?', and your body will respond with answers. These answers will come in the form of symbols, images, and movements.

Enjoy the experience of your inner wisdom.

4

Step Into Expanded Consciousness

4 - Step Into Expanded Consciousness

I Am Vibration

By now you should be ready to expand your being beyond the individual/separate identity you have previously known. This chapter begins by explaining the nature of vibration and then maps out the essentials of a ritual that will literally place you in the centre of the universe, with all the tools necessary, ready to create your world. The rituals and magickal journeys in the following chapters will help you to understand the nature of the vibrational universe in order to attain the divine abilities of conscious creation. Just like the mythical 'God' you will be able to think or speak your world into being. This is Magick in action – the use of ritual and visualisation to influence your deep consciousness, and your beliefs, in such a powerful way that they begin to create a consciously chosen reality (rather than the one you have been accidentally manifesting).

Unfortunately many new students take on rituals without, first of all, developing some self-awareness and clearing away some of the left-over fears and limitations that they have been carrying, and, secondly, without understanding what the rituals and symbols mean. This is dangerous as, without proper knowledge of these powerful principles, things can become very complicated. This chapter will describe the reasoning behind every detail of the rituals, so you can enter the magick with full knowledge and understanding.

The Four (5) Elements

By now, you will be familiar with the concept of vibration through your work with the senses. You may have experienced that you perceive the world of vibration via the senses and that your mind interprets this information based on your beliefs. This chapter will help you understand the magickal concept of vibration, developed by the ancient mystics and magicians across many different cultures, known as the **Four Elements,** and the next chapter will help you get to grips with this on a deep experiential level.

The basic wisdom of the mystics is that **All** is **One** – that is: there is only one vibration/energy that makes up the universe. However, this vibratory energy oscillates at infinitely varying rates. These differences define the 'vibrational states' of the manifest universe. To help our human minds make sense of this, the ancient mystics divided these energies up into the four 'Elements'.

These four Elements have been named: Earth, Water, Fire and Air. These words are not meant as literal descriptions, 'fire' does not simply represent flames or heat, the words are also symbolic representations of the vibrations that are the building blocks of the manifest universe. They are useful to help us conceptualise the nature of this energy. For example, the vibration level of Fire is *like* a flame: quick, changeable, sparky, and unpredictable. Mystics and magicians also work with the concept of a fifth Element, representing the life-force which we call 'Spirit'.

4 - Step Into Expanded Consciousness

In reality there is no division between the Elements, the words are in fact describing a line of continuum from dense/solid/slow to light/free/fast in the following order:

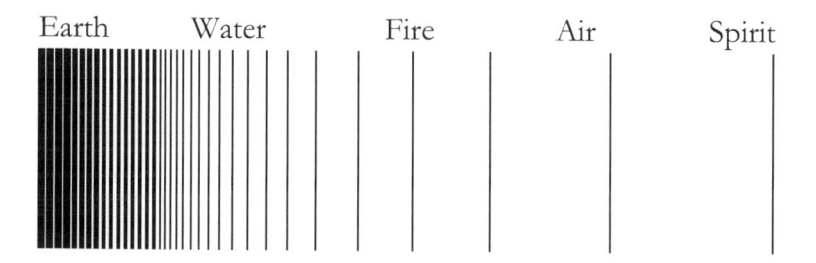

Earth   Water   Fire   Air   Spirit

Rather than describing particular objects, the words describe the 'vibrational state' of the object at a particular moment. Nothing is fixed though – a rock can turn to liquid if enough heat is applied. It is also important to note that when the perspective changes, so too does the appearance of the energy. For example, if I look at a table it looks firm, fixed, solid – very reflective of the Element of 'Earth'. But if I was size of an atom I would be able to see how the atoms of the table, and the electrons within, move around – more akin to the Element of water.

As children we are aware of all levels of vibration – from the most dense and solid to the most subtle. But as people grow older they are often encouraged to only acknowledge the more solid energy that is easily recognised with the 5 Senses (Earth, Water, and Fire). Often recognition of the more subtle energies, which you may know as auras, telepathy, intuition, thought, hunches, or psychic vision etc., is met with suspicion and disdain (due to the influence of religion), even though this recognition is a normal and healthy part of brain function. When children tell their parents about the colours they see around people, the 'fairies', the 'voices', and the 'imaginary' friends, they are often met with fear and told that they are making things up. Over the years they will forget how to 'see' these energies and begin to understand their universe only through the limited vision of the five senses. We learn to see only what we are told is real rather than allowing ourselves to believe the things we perceive, and these subtle energies eventually become invisible to us. However the exercises in the next two chapters will help you to expand your consciousness, reconnecting you with your awareness of the more subtle energies of Air and Spirit.

Following are descriptions of the Elements and also some attributes and magickal symbols that have become associated with them. Words hold us in everyday consciousness by engaging the intellect, but symbols help us to access a deeper place which is essential for magick. The unconscious speaks in symbols, therefore, in order for us to communicate with it, we need to speak in the same language. Symbols are objects or pictures that hold meaning – they represent concepts and experience. Symbols expand meaning, rather than limit it – therefore encouraging access to the creative consciousness. When the magickal symbols of the Elements become familiar to you, they will help you to access the part of your consciousness that relates to the associated vibrational level. Some of the associations are reflected in astrology, the tarot, and other spiritual practices, so you may already be familiar with them.

4 - Step Into Expanded Consciousness

Earth

- ❖ Compass Direction: North – the darkest direction
- ❖ Daily cycle: Night
- ❖ Magickal symbol: Pentacle – a pentagram within a circle
- ❖ Colour: Green
- ❖ Nature: Trees, roots, landscapes, crystals
- ❖ Animals: Earth bound – goats, horses, snakes
- ❖ Mythology: Trolls, elves, minotaur, centaur, giants
- ❖ Tarot suit: Pentacles or Disks (playing cards: clubs)

Properties

The Element of Earth is not to be mistaken for the planet Earth. It is a symbol for the densest vibration. It describes things that are solid, slow, hard, and still. The densest material on Earth is a diamond crystal – its energy is tightly squashed together making it harder and more solid than anything else. Other things that are made up mostly of 'Earth' vibrations are rocks, stones, wood, and metal. But remember, these things only belong in the category of Earth because of their present state of vibration – once a rock becomes molten its vibration changes to that of Water. The Element of Earth represents everything that has a solid form but, also, everything that is similar to the properties of 'solid'. So, for example, animals like elephants, and other slow grazing and heavy animals, are symbolically aligned with this Element.

Personal Reflection

- ❖ **Body** – the vibration of Earth is similar to the hardest parts of our physical body: bones, teeth and nails.
- ❖ **Emotions** – feeling stuck, blocked emotions, feeling centred and calm.
- ❖ **Personality** – strong, assertive, solid, grounded, fixed, having tenacity, being straightforward, stubborn.
- ❖ **Experiences** – the experiences that are similar to Earth vibrations are those which tend to be focused on the physical, or the concerns of the manifest world: home, work, environment, the body in general, and finances.

Water

- ❖ Compass direction: West – where the Sun sets
- ❖ Daily cycle: Evening
- ❖ Magickal symbol: Cup/Chalice
- ❖ Colour: Blue
- ❖ Nature: Rivers, lakes oceans, natural springs
- ❖ Animals: Water based – dolphins, fish, seahorses, turtles, etc.
- ❖ Mythology: Mermaids, water nymphs, Eros, Aphrodite, Cupid
- ❖ Tarot suit: Cups (playing cards: hearts)

Properties

The Element of Water is a symbol describing energy which is less dense than that of Earth. Water represents vibration that is similar to liquid – it moves around, and it is fluid, flowing, malleable, absorbing, seeping, and reflective. Looking to the environment for things that resonate with this energy we find, of course, liquid itself in its many forms (waterfalls, rivers, seas, lakes). Also soft-bodied plants and sea or river animals can share some of the attributes of Water.

Personal Reflection

- ❖ **Body** – liquid or softer body parts such as skin, internal organs, blood.
- ❖ **Emotions** – the emotions that are similar to the Water vibration are love, empathy, care, and emotions that change and reflect. Also, deep

emotions like sadness and grief that overflow and spill out.

- ❖ **Personality** – the personality traits that are similar to Water are: soft, gentle, giving, nurturing, loving, supporting, understanding, changeable, and reflective.
- ❖ **Experiences** – the experiences that are similar to the Water vibration are those which involve joining, sharing, loving, connecting, and reflecting. For example; parent/child relationships, falling in love, and loving sexual connection.

4 - Step Into Expanded Consciousness

Fire

- ❖ Compass direction: South – where the Sun is brightest and hottest
- ❖ Daily cycle: Midday
- ❖ Magickal symbol: Wooden carved stick / magick wand – the fire tool
- ❖ Colour: Red
- ❖ Nature: Volcanoes, lightening strikes, fire itself
- ❖ Animals: Glow worms, lions, fire salamanders
- ❖ Mythology: Dragons, phoenix, pixies
- ❖ Tarot suit: Wands (playing cards: spades)

Properties

The Element of Fire is less dense than Water. It represents the vibration which is the transition between Water and Air. It relates to things like: physical heat, the vibration created when two people feel a spark of passion between them, explosive energy – lightning and thunder for example. Imagine a flame... it is neither liquid nor gas, its energy is changeable and unpredictable, it moves around quickly in all directions, it feels warm/hot, it is bright, it can spark, and it can suddenly engulf or just as suddenly expire.

Personal Reflection

- ❖ **Body** – The areas of the body that relate to Fire are the endocrine system, which controls our hormones and glands, adrenaline, fight or flight

response, intuitive decision-making, re-acting without thinking and sexual responsiveness.
- ❖ **Emotions** – the emotions that reflect Fire are those which come, go, and change quickly. For example: anger, frustration, passion, and lust.
- ❖ **Personality** – the personality types that reflect this energy can be fiery, assertive, passionate, creative, spontaneous, powerful, bossy and aggressive.
- ❖ **Experiences** – the experiences that are associated with this vibration are passionate sex, the creative process, playfulness, intuition, excitable energy, and feeling motivated and 'fired up'.

Air

- ❖ Compass direction: East – where the Sun rises
- ❖ Daily cycle: Morning
- ❖ Magickal symbol: Sword or crystal wand
- ❖ Colour: Yellow
- ❖ Nature: Wind, sky, clouds, breath, mist, sky
- ❖ Animals: Air based – birds, butterflies, flying insects
- ❖ Mythology: Angels, fairies, Pegasus
- ❖ Tarot suit: Swords (playing cards: diamonds)

Properties

To imagine the Element of Air, it is easiest to think of a thin wisp of smoke. Smoke makes the behaviour of Air visible. Air is free, light, mobile, formless, and very easy to change. For example, when you blow gently, even from very far away, the path of the smoke is affected. Air relates to things like sound, smell, the energy of light, microwaves, and colour.

Personal Reflection

- ❖ **Body** – The body reflects the Element of Air when thinking, organising, using the intellect, and communicating.
- ❖ **Emotions** – Air relates more to thought and less to emotion. So the function of emotion that connects with Air vibration is when the emotions are hidden, cut off, or unnecessary.

- ❖ **Personality** – The personality traits that reflect Air are: aloof, cold, fair, thoughtful, direct, distant, and intelligent.
- ❖ **Experiences** – Experiences which connect us to the vibration of Air are: learning, verbal communication, language, reading, fantasising, games such as chess, organising, categorising, concentration, and focus of mind.

4 - Step Into Expanded Consciousness

Spirit

- ❖ Magickal symbol: Globe of light
- ❖ Colour: White

Spirit represents energy that is so subtle that it can only be recognised by the Sixth Sense. It is the vibration of electromagnetic energy, thought transmission, expansive connection, energetic healing, psychic vision, and the immediate vibrations around all objects/beings – sometimes known as 'auras'. Spirit breathes divine energy into the other Elements to create the spark of life. The pentagram (below) is used to symbolise the four Elements and Spirit working together to create a whole. You may be familiar with this sacred shape. However, it has been misused in horror movies to represent 'evil forces' or devil worship and has therefore developed a negative reputation. But this symbol has been used for thousands of years, across many cultures, to represent nature and divinity entwined as one – the magick of creation. Beautiful... Simple.

Understanding Ritual

Every spiritual path requires some kind of ritual. It is absolutely necessary for the training of the mind. In working through this book so far you have experienced meditation and body-based explorations. From this point on you will be working directly with your unconscious, the collective consciousness, and astral journeying techniques in order to gain your knowledge and understanding. For this reason it is important to thoroughly prepare your psyche.

This preparation takes the form of a ritual that utilises the concept of the four Elements, sacred geometry, your body, the space you are in, and your mind. It is called the **ritual of the sacred circle**. The full instructions for this are detailed in the following chapter. It draws on many ancient magickal practices. Once you have mastered this (when it has become second nature and you can accomplish it by simple intention of will) the aim can be achieved in a second, without words or actions. But until then, a powerful ritual is very necessary.

Many pentagram rituals used today are based on Qabalistic, Hermetic, Masonic, Christian, Rosicrucian, and Golden Dawn practices. These rituals often cling to the idea that it is necessary to banish 'evil spirits'. But this comes from a religious viewpoint which battles 'good' against 'evil', due to the fact that the ancient magickal practices were re-established under the umbrella of Christian Gnosticism (mysticism within the Christian framework). In order to 'banish' something, you must first believe that it exists. But

4 - Step Into Expanded Consciousness

'evil' is not a helpful belief to cultivate. It is a construct of the human mind rather than a true reflection of the universe.

Some people who use these rituals hold the mistaken idea that the power of magick is held within the precise text and complicated actions and that one must never stray from them. Although there is power in the words and actions of these rituals, the positive results of any ritual are actually attained using the power of the mind, the belief, and the intention. Without full understanding of the deeper meaning of these old rituals they fail to resonate with the heart or the unconscious and they can feel empty and meaningless.

During my years of magickal experience, I have carefully considered the 'traditional' wording. I have found that much of it is superfluous and much more of it draws from religious sources. However, I have explored the effects of various options and I have created a circle ritual which is more relevant to now. The **ritual of the sacred circle** is free of the need for any belief, dogma, or archaic practice, and it contains only the tools and techniques that are absolutely necessary for useful results.

Ritual of the Sacred Circle – The Function

It is important to know and understand every aspect of ritual before you enter into it. Ritual is very powerful and can move your unconscious in unexpected ways. I explain the aspects of the ritual below. Please take care to make sense of it before you move on. The **ritual of the sacred circle** is a process which shifts the consciousness in preparation for magickal transformation.

1. It works to **alter the state of consciousness** and to quieten the mind.
2. It works to **open the 'mind's eye'** and open to the bigger-self – your inner truth and your wisdom.
3. It works to **enhance awareness of vibration**.
4. It helps you to **practice visualisation**.
5. It practices focus and concentration with the creation and empowerment of **thought-forms**.
6. It enables the practitioner to align with the forces in the universe using **sacred geometry**.

1. Altering the State of Consciousness

Using the EEG (Electroencephalography) machine, invented by the neurologist Hans Berger, different brain states have been measured by recording the fluctuating speeds of the pulses of electrical activity on the scalp. He identified what he called 'alpha' and 'beta' waves ('theta' and 'delta' waves have also since been identified). What neuroscientists have collectively noticed with the EEG is that the normally functioning brain has frequencies which

4 - Step Into Expanded Consciousness

range between 2 and 40 pulses per second. When the brain is more active, the waves become faster. As the activity of the brain quietens the frequency of brainwaves slow down. They have found that:

- We emit <u>beta brainwaves</u> (13 - 40 cycles per second) when we are consciously alert, or when the mind is engaged in mental activity. For example, when using language and the intellect, or when we feel agitated, tense and afraid.
- The <u>alpha brainwaves</u> (8 -13 cycles per second) are reflective of a state of physical and mental relaxation achieved during meditation and resting consciousness. Interestingly, it has been found that this is the ideal condition to learn new information, perform elaborate tasks, learn languages, and analyse complex situations. By quieting the mind it seems that people experience enhanced mental clarity.
- We slow down to <u>theta brainwaves</u> (4 -7 cycles per second) when the conscious mind or ego literally cuts out. This can occur during periods of long driving, repetitive actions, or very deep meditation. Interestingly, the same brain state is associated with extreme trauma or anger (including tantrums in children) – where the mind stops and the body takes over. This state can also be induced during experiences such as: one's own birth, sexual ecstasy, childbirth, near-death, and psychosis.
- <u>Delta brainwaves</u> are the slowest (1/2 to 4 cycles per second). This is the sleep state.

Mystics have always understood that the brain functions differently according to what it is experiencing. These brainwave measurements have been useful in making scientific sense of this. Different ritual and meditation techniques have been used to enter these states by choice.

- ❖ The normal everyday state (beta) is induced simply by engaging with communication, thought, and the external world.
- ❖ A state of calm stillness where the brain is quieter and there are more gaps between thoughts (alpha) is induced using gentle meditation and visualisation, and by simply closing the eyes and focusing on the breath.
- ❖ A timeless, blissful, ecstatic state (theta), where there may be visions, colours, experiences of leaping into another time/space, a disassociation from your physical body, and experiences of your consciousness travelling separately from your body, can be induced by powerful ritual, long and deep breathing, very focused meditation, repeated and rhythmical pain, and consciously-heightened sexual energy. This state also activates the pineal gland (see below).

All of these states can also be induced by listening to sound pulses with the corresponding number of beats per second. Many ritual practices from all over the world include the use of a drum played repetitively to both induce a trance state and also to bring the practitioners back to everyday consciousness. They are very powerful and I encourage you to try meditating and journeying with them.

4 - Step Into Expanded Consciousness

The **ritual of the sacred circle** creates consciousness shifts. Firstly taking you to the alpha level and then, through the repeated actions, words, meditation, and visualisation, the brain will move to the theta level, ready for new patterns to be created. This prepares the brain for the work ahead and, when you have finished, the closing ritual will bring you back to normal everyday consciousness.

2. Open the Mind's Eye

The pineal gland is a single gland in the centre of the brain. It is shaped like a pine-cone, hence its name. It has been known as 'the seat of consciousness' and the 'mind's eye'. The pineal gland has always been understood by mystics to be the access point to the divine. If you look carefully you will see pine-cones all over religious symbolism. The pineal gland, when stimulated, is thought to activate the release of (among other things) a naturally occurring chemical compound known as DMT or Dimethyltryptamine. It has been suggested that its release is also activated during intense trauma and near-death experiences, as people often report visions and/or out-of-body occurrences during these times.

This compound is found everywhere in nature, including within plants and animals, scientist have yet to make sense of why it is so widespread. When harvested or manufactured it can be used as a psychedelic drug. Indigenous shamans have been aware of this for thousands of years, and they use plants containing it to make brews such as ayahuasca for their rituals and journeys. When people ingest it they commonly report experiences of 'suddenly understanding the nature of reality and the universe' and 'a sense of timeless Oneness'. However they can also report 'overwhelming fear', and some find it difficult to reintegrate their intense experiences.

When the pineal gland is stimulated by focused visualisation, and a ritually-induced shift to the theta state, DMT and other chemicals are released and all the experiences above can be entered into in a calm and balanced state of mind. Fear is unnecessary, the experiences can last for as long as you need, and the learning that is achieved will remain with you for the rest of your life. There is no need for trauma, or indeed psychedelics, in order to awaken your mind to these amazing adventures. When the 'mind's eye' is opened through ritual, visualisation, or meditation we have access to, and can interact with, a universe that is far beyond the physical reality.

The **ritual of the sacred circle** involves specific elements that activate the pineal gland ready for the journeys and experiences.

3. Enhancing Awareness of Vibration

The concept of vibration defines the understanding that nothing is ever still. Everything wobbles, gyrates, and dances. Using words, visualisation, and body-wisdom, you will connect with the four Elements and Spirit during the **ritual of the sacred circle**. By stepping into the different levels of vibration with your body and mind you will 'join' each Element one-by-one and resonate with the vibrations. You will come to know the Elements. You will be able to

4 - Step Into Expanded Consciousness

use this knowledge both during your magickal journeys and during everyday life.

4. Practicing Visualisation

By focusing the mind it is possible to consciously create images of your choice and hold them in your imagination. This is an essential skill for the practicing magician. When you are resonating with your divine connection, you will eventually be able to use this skill to create chosen realities. By practicing this repeatedly during the ritual, you will eventually master the act of creation-by-thought.

5. Creating Thought-Forms

A thought-form is a 3-dimensional image (usually of some kind of mythical being) that is fixed in the mind by groups of people (cultures/tribes/religions) while they collude in the belief of its actual existence. They help us to tell stories and evoke emotional responses – fear or excitement for example. Thought-forms can be created from story or fantasy, for example: Santa Claus, fairies, unicorns, and mermaids. Adults often create thought-forms via fairy stories in order to 'protect' children, for example, from going into the woods alone – the big bad wolf in the story of 'Little Red Riding Hood', or to instil Christian ideals, for example, of 'good' versus 'evil' – snow white and the wicked stepmother/witch. They are also used as tools by religious organisations to create myths that will define our beliefs and manipulate our behaviour (God, Allah, angels, and demons, for example).

Thought-forms are embedded in the mind when stories are told during altered states of consciousness. Children up to the age of around six are already mostly in a theta state anyway, but with the added effects of dim lighting and a warm cosy bed, the mind is like a sponge soaking up and believing the information that is given. The candle light, the incense, the beautiful choral music, and the lulling voice of a priest cause religious devotees to drop into very slow alpha states and sometimes theta states of consciousness. Without the (beta) mind to analyse, criticise, and question the information the myths quickly become their reality.

Thought-forms create belief. When something is believed, the unconscious responds accordingly without the interference of the mind. For example, a belief in the 'big bad wolf' will stop a child in its tracks at the entrance to a forest, and a belief in the wrath of God will send 'sinners' into a spiral of self-induced panic – no conscious thought necessary.

When used consciously, thought-forms are extremely helpful. They can be used to create beings who will act as our protectors or guides and can induce feelings of being loved and cared for. A goddess/god-like thought-form can be used as a way to by-pass your ego/little-self in order to communicate with your own divine wisdom. The little-self is not very good at believing in your divinity so it can be easier to project your divinity onto an external 'being' in order to get at the information you already know.

Goddess/god thought-forms can also be re-absorbed into the psyche to help the magician acknowledge their own

4 - Step Into Expanded Consciousness

divine power. It sounds very convoluted but the little-you wants to stay 'little' at all costs and sometimes some self-trickery is necessary. The more often the tricks are used the more the magician can experience the feeling of divine power. Eventually the trickery is unnecessary as new beliefs become deeply instilled.

When working magickally with thought-forms you will be required to literally be in two minds. You will, on the one hand, know that these are imaginative creations but, on the other, you will actively suspend your disbelief and the thought-forms will come to life. Using the same techniques as the magickal rituals seen in churches, you will alter your state of consciousness and bring your thought-forms to life. However, yours will be chosen to empower rather than to disempower you.

The **ritual of the sacred circle** asks you to create thought-forms to represent each of the four Elements. They are used to personify the Elements which will help you to remember what they represent (for example, a floating, intellectual-looking, angelic winged figure for Air). They are often imagined as protectors or holders of the sacred space, watching over you while you surrender to the altered state of consciousness. They can also be invited into your journeys with you. If you feel stuck or scared, they can come and help or advise.

6. Sacred Geometry

The universe is made up of vibration. This vibration arranges itself into patterns and shapes. From our very own DNA to distant spiral galaxies the patterns are the same. All natural repeated patterns become smaller or larger in the same ratio, known as the 'Golden Ratio' or the 'Divine Proportion'. These ratios can be seen in all of nature – for example, in the curve of a spiral shell or in the pattern of seeds on a flower head. They can be seen in the proportions of all life forms, for example, the human face and body, the shape of a dolphin.

There are some simple shapes that are repeated everywhere in nature. Representations of these shapes and ratios are incorporated into the **ritual of the sacred circle**. The ritual makes use of these shapes in order to:

- ❖ Remind you how the universe manifests.
- ❖ Allow you to experience the power of these shapes and dimensions when they work together.
- ❖ Allow you the imagined experience of being in the centre of the universe.
- ❖ Remind you of the ingredients of creation.
- ❖ Give you practice in taking control of your universe by directing the pure aspects of life, so you can experience your ability to create and manipulate the energies in the universe.
- ❖ Align with the workings of the universe in order to know it (the macrocosm) and therefore yourself (the microcosm).

During the ritual, you will be asked to visualise:

0. **The circle.** This shape will be drawn around the outside of your working space by candle light. This is the energy of 'no-thing' – the place beyond manifestation. Drawing the circle reminds your

4 - Step Into Expanded Consciousness

consciousness that you will be going into silence, the place between thought, and the place of meditation. Drawing a circle around yourself also speaks to your unconscious about the idea of a safe and sacred space, giving you permission to go deeper.

1. **The point.** Representing the beginning or the seed of everything. During the ritual you will roll your eyes up inside your head and look at the six-pointed star, which is resting on the very tip of a pyramid (the single point). This awakens the pineal gland.

2. **The line.** You will visualise two triangles travelling towards each other in a straight line – one from above and one from below. This represents the connection between the manifest and the un-manifest, between our physical and astral body, and between the worlds of the seen and the unseen – suggesting to the unconscious that you wish to make this link.

3. **The triangle.** The upward pointing triangle represents the earth and the aspirations towards spirit, the downward pointing triangle represents spirit and the aspirations towards manifestation.

4. **The square.** As you walk around the circle you will face the four compass directions, creating a square – the base of the pyramid. This represents solidity and strength, and the reality of the physical world.

5. **The pentagram.** At each compass point, you will draw a five-pointed star or pentagram. This represents the four directions connecting with spirit all working together to create life. It also represents the human form in balance, purity, and harmony.

6. **The hexagram.** As above, so below. Having watched the two triangles travelling towards each other you will then visualise them meeting and crossing each other to create a six-pointed star. This is a symbol of the manifest and the un-manifest becoming one – I am All!

Pyramid Power

The final and most powerful aspect of this ritual is to visualise a pyramid surrounding you.

The pyramid is one of the most powerful and healing sacred shapes. It has a square base and four triangles. Energy can move from the tip of the pyramid and spread down to the base, or it can move up from the base, contracting the energy into the single point at the top.

The pyramid was used in many ancient cultures. It has been found to have amazing healing and balancing properties. Visualising it around you will connect you with all its magickal and inter-dimensional power.

It is not particularly important what the pyramid is made from (stone, metal, cardboard, or wood) it will still have the same powerful properties. In the ritual, the pyramid is

4 - Step Into Expanded Consciousness

defined with the mind – a thought-form. Even though it is a non-physical pyramid it is still extremely powerful.

With the **ritual of the sacred circle** finished, you will be sitting in the centre of the universe complete with all the powers and energies in existence ready to create and manifest, and ready to transform from little-you into the powerful being that you are.

5

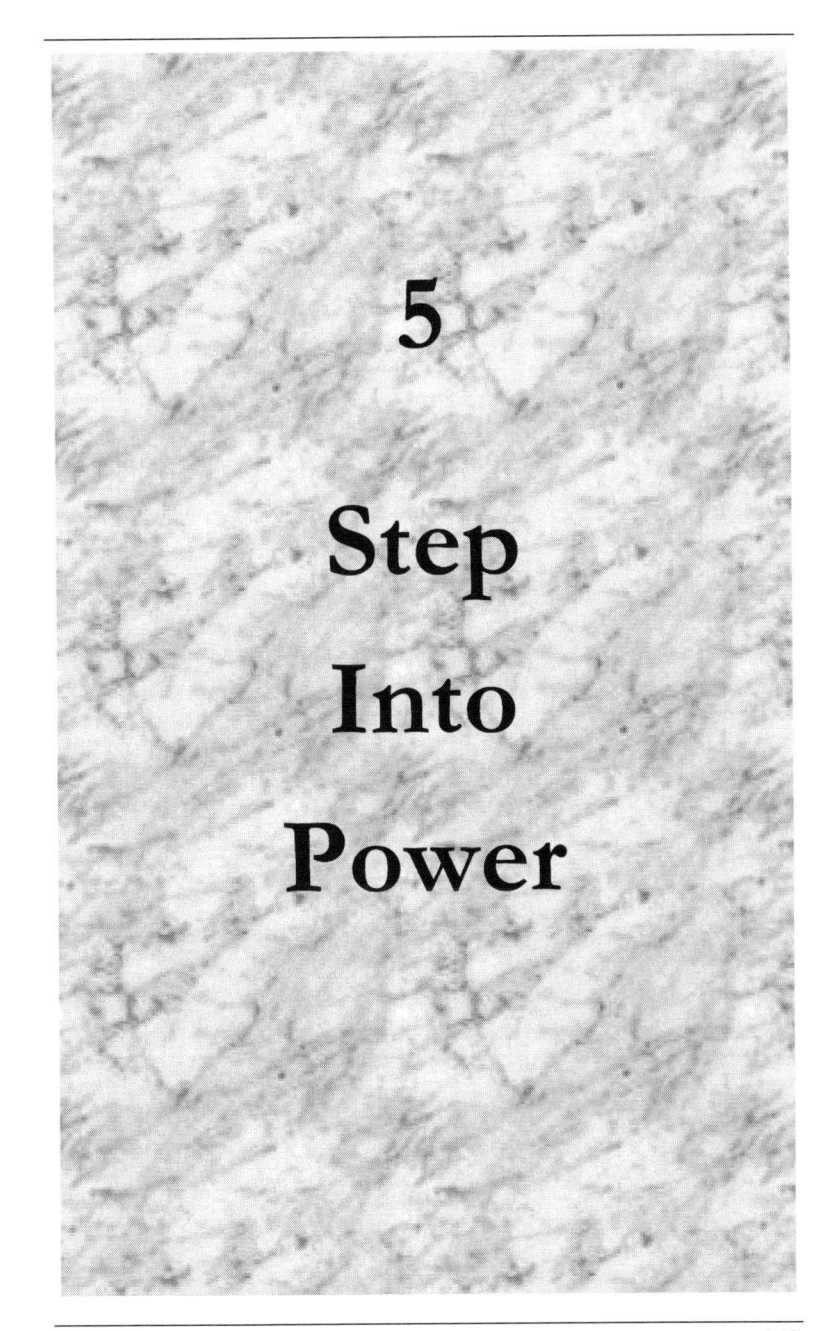

Step Into Power

5 - Step Into Power

Awakening to Ritual

The ritual offered here is based on ancient and present-day practice and personal experience. It is stripped of unnecessary and complicated jargon, and everything in the ritual is relevant to the purpose. Here you have everything necessary to raise the consciousness and prepare the mind for transformational and magickal work. When the circle is raised you will be in a space that is empowered with every force in the universe. Using the power of sacred geometry, which reflects the manifesting power of the universe, together with the visualising power of the mind, and the thought-forms of the Elements, you will potentially be in a position to heal, transform, and create anything.

The **ritual of the sacred circle** is an extremely powerful ritual and should be performed with reverence and with understanding of all the elements within it. Please make sure you have read the previous chapter before performing this ritual. With regular practice this ritual prepares your emotional, mental, intuitive, spiritual, and physical being. Over time, and with familiarity, it will become second nature for you to find yourself in the perfect state of mind to work magickally. Eventually you will have no need for the full ritual or even any ritual at all because it will have become part of you. You will be so ready to step into your divine consciousness that a particular word or a thought will take you there. It is repeated in appendix 1 and 2. I have also included a condensed version of the ritual (appendix 3) for times when you are away from home or when you are short of time. But this should only be used once you are familiar with the full length ritual.

Clothing

You may find it useful to find some special clothes which you use only for transformational work although nakedness is a perfect option. Natural fabrics are perfect, but find for yourself what works best. Choose colours that you love or that express your magickal self. Make sure they're comfortable enough to sit in your meditation posture. If you can, choose or make clothing that helps you to feel a sense of ceremony – such as a robe or a long dress or kaftan.

Cleansing

Cleansing both your mind and body is of utmost importance. During ritual cleansing you will wash away all the stresses and tensions which have accumulated during your everyday activities. You are also working to separate your mundane existence from your magickal life. Anything that needs to be washed away during the cleansing ritual can be seen as a veil over your inner being. This veil is useful in your daytime life as it helps you to stay in touch with the everyday reality. But it needs to be removed in order to work with the astral reality. Over time you will find that your spiritual self can easily become part of your everyday self. Your little-you voice will diminish and you will begin to live your truth at all times, and you won't need the veil anymore. You will be capable of walking in both worlds at the same time. Therefore the cleansing is not essential forever, but you may find it useful at first.

5 - Step Into Power

Light a candle and thoughtfully remove your daytime clothing. Step into the shower or bath and wash if you need to. Now close your eyes and focus on the sensation of the water on your skin. Imagine all the stresses of the day coming to the surface of your skin and being rinsed or soaked away by the water. Release physical tension and be aware of the sensation of letting go. Have a sense of the water dissolving all the little-you fears, and give yourself some love. Breathe deeply and steadily as you are doing this. You are looking for a steady settling of energy and for a sense of balance and calm. When you feel soft, clear and relaxed, dry yourself and dress in your ritual clothing.

Establish Thought-Forms

As you know by now, the unconscious understands and communicates in the language of symbol. Therefore, when you are performing this ritual, it is important to not only speak the words but to use your imagination and visualisation skills as well. In the circle you will be creating thought-forms of each of the Elements.

When you can eventually let go of the fact that they are simply projected aspects of your own unconscious, these thought forms will take the shape of beings with their own will. Your thought-forms don't have to be human, but it is important that they take the shape of something that can communicate clearly with you. Don't worry if you're not sure whether it is the correct image for you, whatever you choose will develop as you get to know it.

- ❖ **Earth thought-form**

    Think about all the properties of the Element of Earth (solid, physical, strong, etc.) and imagine a being that personifies this energy. You can use images from mythology or you can use a simple symbol. For example: a person sitting on a solid wooden throne which has roots that reach deep into the earth, a tree-being, a minotaur or centaur, a gnome or troll. Also, visualise the environment surrounding the thought-form, and be very aware of your physical body when you connect with your Earth Spirit. Use plenty of green in the picture – in order to vibrate with the same energy.

- ❖ **Water thought-form**

    Remember all you know about the Element of Water (flowing, seeping, reflective, emotional flow, deep emotion, love etc.) and allow an image to come to mind. Some examples of the Spirit of Water are: a person standing underneath a waterfall, a being made of water, a dolphin, a mermaid, or a water nymph. Allow the Water Spirit to raise feelings of flowing openness and love. Visualise the landscape surrounding your Water Spirit, and vibrate the colour blue.

5 - Step Into Power

❖ **Fire thought-form**

> Your Spirit of Fire will be dynamic, full of spark and passion. An example could be a being made of fire and dancing like the flames. It might be a dragon or a phoenix leaping from the flames, or an angel of fire. This being should raise your passion and creative energy. You should feel ready for action when working with your Fire Spirit, and you should feel the energy in your body. Visualise a fiery landscape, and vibrate the colour red.

❖ **Air thought form**

> Your spirit of Air needs to clear your mind and to raise a sense of sharpness and intellect, while at the same time connecting you with a meditative state. It could be a wispy floating being or an intelligent-looking angel with huge white wings. You may prefer to use the image of a butterfly or a wise owl, a sharp eyed eagle or a fairy with delicate wings. Visualise an airy landscape (sky, clouds etc.) and vibrate the colour yellow.

Whatever you choose for each Element, it is important that you have positive feelings towards your thought-forms as they will become your allies on your astral journeys

Make the Ritual your Own

It is helpful for you to use the **ritual of the sacred circle** for any magickal or transformational work. The complete ritual is extremely powerful and you will gain a huge amount from performing it. It will serve to speak to you on a symbolic level in order to create a bridge between the conscious and unconscious parts of your mind. It will help you move from an everyday awareness into magickal/astral consciousness in order to travel to other dimensions.

The more you perform this ritual the more powerful it will become. Before you begin you may wish to practice drawing pentagrams with a pen and paper. You may also find it helpful to use your body in order to help you connect with the energies of each Element in a physical way – holding your arms out towards the directions, for example. You could also dance or choose a specific movement for each Element. When you are more practiced, it should take around 5 to 10 minutes for you to perform.

You will need:

- ❖ Your special clothing.
- ❖ A minimum of one candle, or one each of yellow, red, blue, and green in holders which reflect the corresponding Elements.
- ❖ An object to represent each of the four Elements. Place each object as a marker for the associated direction. From now on, the objects must only be used for magickal purposes such as ritual or healing. This will help your unconscious to easily

5 - Step Into Power

recognise the objects as symbols of a ritual space with a magickal purpose, and will eventually start to trigger the state of mind necessary. Some traditional examples of Elemental symbols are:

- Air – East: sword, feather, quill pen.
- Fire – South: a wand carved from wood, a beautiful stick.
- Water – West: a chalice, a bowl of water.
- Earth – North: a large disk with a pentagram carved on it or a pentagram within a circle known as a 'pentacle', or a large stone.

You may also wish to decorate small altars in each of the four directions, placing special objects, fabric, and candles relating to each Element.

Begin the ritual by facing the easterly direction and follow the instructions for the calling of Air. Then move around the circle facing each of the four directions and following the instructions. This creates the astral circle, the square, and the pentagram, and begins the process of raising your consciousness. The final part – calling on your higher power – brings in the line, the point, the triangle, the six-pointed star (or hexagram), and finally the pyramid.

This begins the process of activating your pineal gland and opening the gateway to visions and experiences that you would not have in everyday consciousness. You can use the words suggested here or write your own, bearing in mind the intention behind the ritual. When you speak, aim to resonate your voice with a deeper pitch and speak more slowly than you normally would. Or you could sing or chant the words. This allows the words to vibrate into your body and into your space. Try to find the meaning in your body and be aware of the emotional response to the words you are saying.

I have pointed out the directions to draw each Elemental pentagram. If you prefer to keep it simple, just use the Earth pentagram for each quarter.

The Ritual of the Sacred Circle

Call the Spirit of Air

- ❖ Face the East.
- ❖ Light the yellow candle, or your single white candle, and hold it up.
- ❖ Inhale the energy of the Element Air.
- ❖ Hold awareness of your intellect and your mind, and smile to lighten your thoughts.
- ❖ Visualise your Air thought-form facing you and say:

"Spirit of Air,
bringing life and light from the East.
You who offer clarity of mind,
focused thought,
and open the doors to clear communication.
The eagle, the hummingbird, and the fairies.
The wide open skies, the soft clouds,
and the air I breathe.
Be here this day.
Let darkness and light reside in balance
and harmony.
Welcome Spirit of Air"

I Am God

- ❖ Draw the Air pentagram with your candle (by drawing the first line towards Air as shown above, and as in the diagram on page 147), by doing this you are inviting Air energy into your space.
- ❖ Walk around the room clockwise drawing a large circle with the candle. Imagine that you are drawing the energy of Air around you.
- ❖ Put down the candle at the Air altar and pick up your chosen Air object. Hold it with intent, facing the East, and say:

> *"Let this… (put the name of your object here – 'cup', 'chalice' etc.)… be filled with the power of Air"*

- ❖ When you do this you are empowering your object as a symbol so your unconscious will begin to associate it with meaning. It may be useful for you during a journey.
- ❖ Place it down again.

5 - Step Into Power

Call the Spirit of Fire

- ❖ If you have just one candle carry it to the Fire altar. If you have a different candle in each quarter, take the Fire candle and light it from the Air candle.
- ❖ Turn to face the South.
- ❖ Hold up the candle.
- ❖ Inhale the energy of Fire.
- ❖ Feel your passion and creative flow and smile to bring sparkles to your body.
- ❖ Visualise your thought-form for Fire facing you and say:

> *"Spirit of Fire,*
> *bringing warmth and health from the South.*
> *You who offer passion, creative energy,*
> *and open the doors to intuition.*
> *The salamander, the phoenix,*
> *and the dragon.*
> *The heat of the sun, the warmth of the*
> *hearth, and the pleasure in my belly.*
> *Be here this day.*
> *Let darkness and light reside in balance*
> *and harmony.*
> *Welcome Spirit of Fire"*

I Am God

- ❖ Draw the Fire pentagram with your candle, the first line going towards Fire (as above).
- ❖ Walk around the room clockwise, drawing a circle with the candle. Imagine that you are drawing the power of Fire around you.
- ❖ Put down the candle at the Fire altar and pick up your chosen Fire object. Hold it with intent, still facing the South, and say:

> *"Let this... (name your object)... be filled with the power of Fire"*

- ❖ Place your object down again.

5 - Step Into Power

Call the Spirit of Water

- ❖ If you have just one candle, carry it to the Water altar. If you have a different candle in each quarter, take the Water candle and light it from the Fire candle.
- ❖ Face the West.
- ❖ Hold up the candle.
- ❖ Inhale the energy of Water.
- ❖ Feel your emotion and flow, and smile to bring softness to your heart.
- ❖ Visualise your Water thought-form facing you and say:

"Spirit of Water,
bringing love and union from the West.
You who offer emotional flow,
psychic vision,
and open the doors to deep connection.
The dolphins, the mermaids,
and the water nymphs.
The tidal shifts, the ripples on the lakes,
and the deep love in my heart.
Be here this day.
Let darkness and light reside in balance
and harmony.
Welcome spirit of Water"

- ❖ Draw the Water pentagram with your candle, the first line going towards Water (as above).
- ❖ Walk around the room clockwise, drawing a circle with your candle. Imagine that you are drawing the energy of Water around the circle.
- ❖ Put the candle down at the Water altar and pick up your Water object. Hold it with intent towards the west.

> *"Let this... (name your object)... be filled with the power of Water"*

- ❖ Place your object down again.

5 - Step Into Power

Call the Spirit of Earth

- ❖ If you have a single candle, carry it to the Earth altar. If you have a different candle in each quarter, take the Earth candle and light it from the Water candle.
- ❖ Face the North.
- ❖ Hold up the candle.
- ❖ Breathe in the energy of Earth.
- ❖ Feel your feet firmly grounded and connected with the planet Earth.
- ❖ Visualise your thought-form for the Element of Earth facing you and say:

> *"Great Spirit of Earth,*
> *Bringer of the mountains and the trees from the North.*
> *You who offer my food, my home,*
> *and open the doors to the manifest world.*
> *The four footed beasts, the goat,*
> *and the centaur.*
> *The earth beneath me, the life around me,*
> *and my own sensual body.*
> *Be here this day.*
> *Let darkness and light reside in balance and harmony.*
> *Welcome spirits of Earth"*

I Am God

- ❖ Draw the Earth pentagram with your candle. The first line is drawn towards Earth (as above).
- ❖ Walk around the room clockwise, drawing a circle with the candle. Imagine that you are drawing the energy of Earth around the circle.
- ❖ Put down the candle and pick up your Earth object. Hold it with intent towards the North and say:

> *"Let this… (name your object)… be filled with the power of Earth"*

- ❖ Place your object down again.
- ❖ If you have just one candle, walk back to the Eastern quarter and place it there to complete the circle.
- ❖ If you have four candles, walk to the Eastern candle and touch the two flames together to complete the circle. Then place the green candle back on the Earth altar.

5 - Step Into Power

Call the Centre

Close your eyes and visualise the circle of shimmering white light around you. Visualise the pentagrams where you drew them in the air with the candle flames and your thought-form Spirits of Earth, Water, Fire, and Air standing (or floating) in their directions.

Now visualise two triangles, one with its base on the ground pointing upwards (representing all that is manifest), the other high above you pointing downwards (representing all that is non-manifest). Then visualise them moving towards each other in a straight line until they meet at a point just above the centre of the circle creating a six-pointed star. Roll your eyes up inside your head and watch as it glows with golden light. Contemplate the manifest and the non-manifest becoming one.

As the star lights up, visualise a great pyramid surrounding you – the star at its apex. Your visualisation should look a little like the image below. As you stand inside the pyramid feel your feet at its base and visualise your roots stretching deep into the planet Earth. Then raise your arms above your head, pointing to the top of the pyramid, and visualise your fingers growing into roots which reach up into the sky, out into the solar system, further out into the greater cosmos, and then deep into the infinite universes.

At this point, feel yourself opening to all possibilities, imagine yourself in a gap of silence, between words, between thought, and open yourself to cosmic consciousness.

I Am God

Say:

*"In the centre of the great pyramid,
below me the Earth and above me the sky.
Around me the flaming pentagrams and the
circle of light.
Above me the six-rayed star.
This place is sealed."*

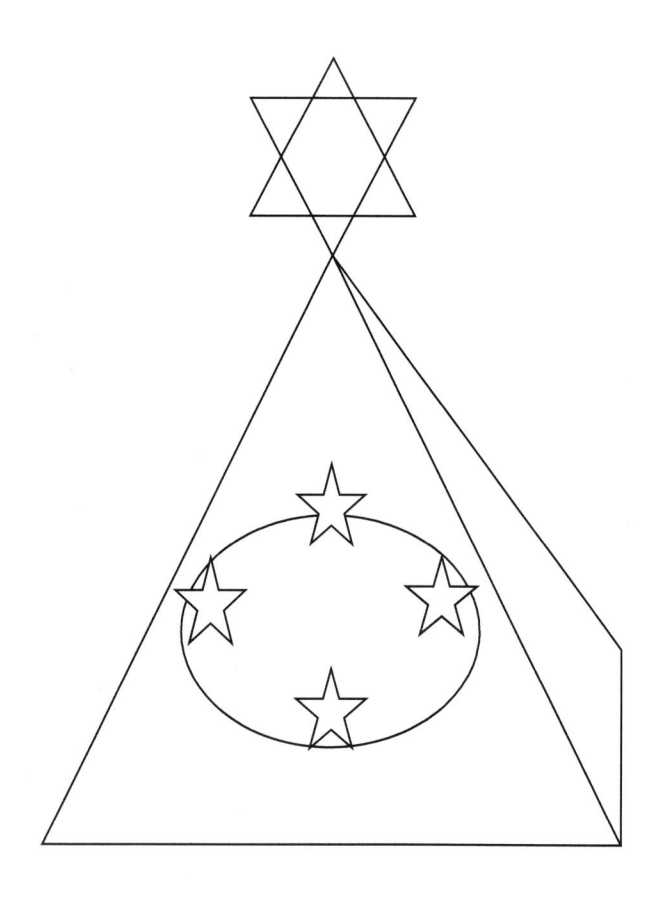

5 - Step Into Power

Call the Higher Power – Spirit

This higher power could be visualised as a light, a shining and loving version of yourself, or a beautiful light-filled and benevolent being. Or you may prefer to focus on a sensation of connection between your physical body and the whole of the universe instead.

The work of mysticism is not about looking up to 'higher' gurus, gods, or goddesses. It is about discovering the vast wealth of knowledge and power you have <u>within you</u> as a divine being. Therefore, if you choose to use a figure, it is important to remember that it is a projected image of your higher being – it is YOU in full attainment. This thought-form is your personal symbol in recognition of your enlightened self – the highest potential of your spiritual being, and the source of all things. In this part of the ritual you are connecting with, and calling on, your divine consciousness. Feel free to change the words as you choose. Raise your arms up, breathe deeply, and say:

> *"Divine Spirit within and without.*
> *I – all of nature and the universe.*
> *I – all Power. I – all creation. I – all Love.*
> *Lead me to wisdom and understanding.*
> *Lead me to do my work and realise my full*
> *potential – to live and serve my divine truth.*
> *Welcome Divine Spirit"*

Sit down in your space, breathe, and hold awareness of your personal divinity.

Now you can start your magickal work.

Release the Circle

At the end of any magickal work it is important to open the circle. This allows your unconscious to recognise that it is time to <u>focus on the manifest world</u>.

*

No matter how successful you are in astral flight, your true measure of enlightenment rests on your success in negotiating the people, the things, the emotions and the interactions of the physical reality. This is the place where you get to practice really living the truth of your divine presence.

*

Face the centre and say:

> *"Great divine spirit within and without.*
> *I thank you for being here with me this day.*
> *I thank you for offering me the wisdom and the understanding to do my work,*
> *To know, in order to serve truth.*
> *Until I call again,*
> *Hail and farewell"*

Visualise your divine spirit, and then watch as it, and the sacred shapes, dissipate into the vibrational surroundings. Extinguish the candles, starting with the Air candle and moving around the circle clockwise. As you do this visualise your spirit of each Element bowing to acknowledge their departure and feel a strong sense of gratitude. Then say:

> *"Open may this circle be"*

5 - Step Into Power

Explore the Astral World

The astral world occupies the same space as the manifest world it simply vibrates at a different frequency. Having raised the circle, your consciousness is prepared to move within this level of reality. The vibrations of the astral world are interpreted via imagination, fantasy, symbols, psychic vision, archetypes, stories, 'hunches', and intuition. The more you resonate with the astral world during your magickal work the more you become open to it in the everyday reality. For example, you may find yourself walking home and having an insight about some future event, or during a woodland walk you may experience a darting, flashing energy amongst the trees.

The astral world is very useful for growth and transformation as it surpasses the limitations of the physical and sensual 'reality'. It is important to note that:

*

The mind does not know the difference between information it receives via the five senses and information it receives via the imagination.

*

For example when you dance your muscles respond by helping you move your body physically, but if you imagine you are dancing your brain will still send information to your muscles – you may even feel them twitching if the electrical impulses are strong enough. In the physical world you cannot fly, but if you imagine you are flying your brain will perceive this information and send the impulses to your body as if it were physically true. In this way, when you experience your reality through dreaming, imagination, or astral travel and allow yourself to explore freely, without limiting your possibilities, you are offering your consciousness new learning, new experience, new potential, new opportunity and, therefore, new growth.

In the astral world your personal boundaries are not limited by your physical body and your knowledge is not limited by your physical brain. Astral travel is the gateway to the collective consciousness. All moments of learning, thought, and experience from all forms of life and existence are here. In the astral world you are connected to this knowledge of All – here you have the answers to every question.

Astral Travel – Journey to Other Realms

There are many different ways to connect with the astral world. In this book the principle method used will be astral travelling, sometimes known as visualisation, quantum leaping, or journeying. During astral travel you can potentially explore and heal many different areas.

- ❖ **Your personal unconscious** – the ego, your memory (including repressed memory, genetic memory, fear, and trauma), your lifelong personal learning and experience, your past dreams and imaginings, genetic memory, intuition, and past or future life memories.
- ❖ **The collective consciousness** – connection with other minds – human, animal, or otherwise. You

5 - Step Into Power

may connect with different energies and other realities, or you may draw on knowledge from other worlds and other beings.

❖ **Divine consciousness** – here you may experience feelings of expansiveness or unity, and connection with the universe and with your own divinity. You may experience feelings of absolute love and fulfilment and other blissful and ecstatic states. You may experience a sense of the knowledge of All.

When astral travelling, the experiences you have can be consciously directed or can be experienced passively – usually a bit of both. You will obtain knowledge and information through symbols, pictures, sensations, and stories much like when you are dreaming. You may be 'visited' by people whose physical lives have ended. You may have 'conversations' with other human figures, animals, plants, rocks, other beings, or mythical beings. Whether you are connecting with projected aspects of your own inner world, external astral beings, or universal consciousness is up to you to decide. The instructions will lead you to a specific astral environment which will resonate with a specific area within your psyche. Once you have arrived take the opportunity to explore and discover.

Some of these beings may become a regular feature and act as guardians or guides on your journeys. These encounters can be useful if you need the answer to a particular question and you have not yet fully integrated the little-you consciousness. Instead of just asking yourself (which of course you could) you can ask the symbols or beings you meet, bypassing the 'little-you' mind. Some of the above may seem far-fetched but, if you can put your disbelief to one side, your experiences will offer you new opportunities for growth and wisdom.

When working with astral travel it is even more important to keep a record of your transformational experience. This will give you an opportunity to look back and compare your journeys. It is not important that you understand the reason behind every image. All of the experiences you have will work towards your healing and growth without the need for intellectual understanding (although some meanings may be obvious). When journeying, some things you experience will act as a clearing or healing process, helping you let go of past memories, habits, and trauma, some things will be messages from your unconscious, and some may be messages from the collective consciousness or your higher self. It is unnecessary to attempt to make logical sense for the work to be successful. Your unconscious will do the work for you.

Astral Journeys to the Vibrational Elements

It is valuable to journey to the four Elements. Not only will you begin to feel and experience how these Elemental ingredients are mixed together to create life but these journeys can also be used to heal specific areas of your psyche, e.g. the journey to Water could help you work on emotional blocks. These journeys will also help you resonate with the Elements more completely when you perform the **ritual of the sacred circle**.

5 - Step Into Power

In the following astral journeys you will explore the four Elements separately and then, in a final journey to the Element of Spirit, you will understand how the vibrations work together. Be aware at all times that these journeys are YOUR experience. You are in full control of events as they happen. If you find an image or experience disturbing and you feel unable to cope with it feel free to change it or to do something differently. Or you may prefer to call on your Elemental Spirits to guide, advise, and protect you. It is very useful to stay with experiences, rather than push them away, in order to work with the areas in your psyche that they represent, but not to the point where you are too frightened to do anything about it. Remember, it is YOUR experience. If something is scary, perhaps visualise yourself flying above it or overpowering it. Explore new ways of dealing with scary events. Remain in your power at all times. This will not only help you heal past events but it will give you new tools for current fearful experiences in the everyday world.

I would advise that you limit your journeys to once-per-week. This will give your unconscious time to integrate the new learning.

To Begin Every Journey

*Perform the **ritual of the sacred circle**. Then sit down in your meditation position. Try to avoid leaning or resting against anything. You may find this difficult at first but it is worth persevering as it will leave your spine free to move if necessary. You may occasionally feel energetic impulses coursing up and down your spine if it is free to respond.*

*Start with the **foundation breath meditation** and then, with your eyes closed, begin to visualise yourself in the room that is around you. See the candles and your altars. Now widen your awareness to include the astral space and visualise the circle of light surrounding you, the pentagrams in the four directions, your thought-form for each of the Spirits of Earth, Water, Fire, and Air. Visualise the pyramid surrounding you and the six-pointed star above you – at the apex of the pyramid. As you roll your eyes up inside your head to look at the six-pointed star you can feel your connection to Divine Spirit. Feel your physical body strong and grounded. As you breathe deeper, become aware of your astral body. Feel its vibration as lighter and freer than your physical body.*

Now let go of the image of the physical objects around you and focus only on the astral shapes and the thought-forms. Next, leaving your physical body where it is, allow your astral body to stand up in your sacred circle and visualise all the sacred shapes surrounding you. Slowly allow all this to fade. Then follow the instructions for the journeys.

5 - Step Into Power

To End Every Journey

When the images of the journey fade, you find yourself standing once again in your room. Let the images of the astral shapes fade also and begin to notice again the material objects in your room. You can see your physical body sitting in the space. As you watch, your physical body breathes, and you feel drawn towards it.

With each breath you feel more and more connected and you allow yourself to fully re-enter your physical body. As you breathe, you begin to feel the breath moving your body and you can feel the weight of your body against the floor or the chair. When you are ready, take three deep, energising and awakening breaths and open your eyes. Then follow the instructions to **release the circle**.

Journey to Earth
30 minutes

Perform the **ritual of the sacred circle,** the **foundation breath meditation** and follow the instructions **to begin every journey** (see appendix 1).

Say:

"Home
Within and Without
Waiting for Growth
Earning Knowledge
Keeping Silence"

When the image of your room and the astral circle fades you find yourself standing in woodland. The trees have strong solid trunks and deep green leaves. It is late evening and you can feel a cool breeze on your skin as the sun is setting. As it grows darker you become aware of the sounds of the night animals.

You begin to pick your way through the trees until you find yourself on a clear pathway. The pathway leads deeper into the woods where the trees are thicker and the woodland denser. Up ahead you notice some large rocks set deep into the earth. You can just make out what looks like a cave entrance in one of the rocks. You continue to follow the pathway and it leads you directly to the cave.

When you arrive at the entrance you take a last look behind you at the forest then you enter. You find a

5 - Step Into Power

tunnel there and tentatively step deeper inside. The air is thick and the rocks are cold to the touch. You follow the tunnel. The way is easy, although you find that you occasionally have to squeeze your way through narrower sections.

You soon find yourself in a large underground cavern. The floor of the cavern is made up of mostly flat rocks, but one of the rocks in the centre has a hollow. It seems to be about your size and shape. It looks like it would fit you very well. You have an urge to climb inside it. You follow this urge and curl up inside the space. As you lie there, feeling held and supported by the rock, you become aware that you are moving. You feel yourself sinking into the ground. As you move deeper, you catch a glimpse of your Spirit of Earth looking down at you.

Here's where I'll leave you to explore... (20 minutes)

When you have finished your explorations, find your way back to your place in the hollow of the rock. You climb out and stand up. Then you give thanks to those who helped you on your journey. You begin to walk back through the tunnel, heading in the direction that you came. You soon find yourself at the cave entrance once again, feeling energised and safe. Finding your path back through the forest, you begin to follow it. Eventually you recognise your starting point, and, when you arrive there, slowly allow the image to fade.

Follow the instructions to **end the journey** *and* **release the circle** *(appendix 2).*

Journey to Water
30 minutes

Follow the instructions in appendix 1 to begin.

Say:

*"Soft Invitation,
Crystal Clear,
Deep, Mysterious...
A Single Tear."*

You find yourself in a meadow sitting by a river. It is late afternoon. The light of the low Sun is reflected on the water's surface. It sparkles like cut jewels. As you watch, you find yourself hypnotised by the patterns it creates. The sound of the water running quickly over the rocks deepens your sense of relaxation. As you gaze further into its depths, you feel compelled to be under the water, and to be washed by the colourful sensual liquid.

You remove your clothing and step into the cool, soft water. You feel it immediately curling around you and caressing you. It feels to you as if the water wants to pull you down. You sense that it wants you to be inside it. As you immerse your body further you feel held and comforted.

You surrender to the water. You no longer need to think. The water pulls you down, it shapes itself around you. You let go of control. The water has taken

5 - Step Into Power

you. You feel loved and wanted and you experience a deep inner cleansing.

You begin to realise that you are travelling with the river. You can feel the bends and turns of its path. Become aware of your Spirit of Water swimming with you.

Here's where I'll leave you to explore... (20 minutes)

When you feel ready, find your way back to the river and begin to swim gently towards your starting point. The river helps you with this. When you arrive there, give thanks to those who helped you during your journey and climb out of the water and back onto the riverbank.

Slowly the images begin to fade.

Follow the instructions in appendix 2 to finish.

Journey to Fire
30 minutes

Follow the instructions in appendix 1 to begin.

Say:

*"Passions Blazing
Inspire Creation.
Conception Invented,
Wildness Unsated."*

You find yourself walking in a desert. It is mid afternoon and the Sun is high in the sky. The sand is hot under your feet and you can feel the heat of the sun on your skin.

As you walk you can hear the loud crackling sound of distant flames. You look up and can see a raging fire ahead. You continue to walk and, as you move closer, you begin feel the heat of the fire on your skin.

The sound becomes louder and the heat continues to grow in intensity. When you arrive there you see your Spirit of Fire standing inside the flames. You stand and look into the fire. You can see the patterns of orange, white, red, and yellow dancing together, and you can feel the heat against your skin.

The fire somehow looks inviting. Your Spirit of Fire smiles and beckons you towards the flames. You feel safe as you begin to step forwards into the raging heat. Your Spirit of Fire encourages you further inside.

5 - Step Into Power

Here's where I'll leave you to explore... (20 minutes)

When your journey has come to an end, bring yourself back to the fire and step out of the flames. Stand by the side of the fire once again. Give thanks to those who helped you on your journey and begin to make your way back across the desert, following the footprints you made on the way here. You soon find yourself at your starting point and slowly the images begin to fade.

Follow the instructions in appendix 2 to finish.

Journey to Air
30 minutes

Follow the instructions in appendix 1 to begin.

Say:

*"Clarity of Vision
Blows My Mind.
Shining Thoughts Sparkle
Like Clouds Glistening in Reflection"*

You find yourself standing in a meadow. It is early morning, the Sun is shining, and you can feel a light breeze on your skin. The sky above is bright blue with the occasional cloud floating gently along. There are birds flying above and you can hear the morning chorus as they begin their day. The air feels fresh, cool and nurturing in your lungs, and you breathe it hungrily.

In the distance you can hear the sound of crashing waves. You begin to walk towards the sound, enjoying the lightness of your footsteps on the soft, cool, dewy grass. Your walk is brisk and you are moving quickly and easily.

The land begins to rise ahead of you and you walk up the slight incline. As you walk higher, your breath comes faster and stronger.

You begin to increase your speed in order to reach the top quickly. You begin to run. The last few steps are so fast that you close your eyes to enjoy the sensation.

5 - Step Into Power

Suddenly the ground disappears from under your feet. You look down and you realise that you now are flying above the sea. Behind you is the cliff-face from which you leapt. As you settle into your flight, you feel the presence of your Spirit of Air flying with you.

Here's where I'll leave you to explore... (20 minutes)

When you feel ready, find your way back to the cliff and gently place your feet on the ground. Look back at where you've been and give thanks to those who helped you on your journey. Make your way back down the hill to the meadow. You soon find yourself back at your starting point and slowly the images begin to fade.

Follow the instructions in appendix 2 to finish.

Journey to Spirit
30 minutes

This is a visualisation which explores all the Elements and Spirit together. Through this you will discover how the building blocks of life and yourself come together, how things are made, how things are manifested and created in your universe, and how things can easily change from one vibration to another.

Follow the instructions in appendix 1 to begin.

You find yourself in a tunnel. You look around at your new environment. You reach out your hand and touch stone walls. They are slightly damp and cold. Lanterns placed against the wall at intervals light your way. You follow the tunnel through twists and turns. It seems infinitely long. You are just beginning to consider turning back when you notice that the tunnel is beginning to widen.

You walk a little quicker and, as you round the next corner, you find yourself in a small cavern. There are fire lanterns on the walls. In the centre of the cavern is a large square wooden table. On the table are your four symbolic objects which represent the Elements. In the centre is your symbol for the fifth Element of Spirit. You pick up each object in turn. As you do this, you feel its energy coursing through your body. Each elemental symbol affects you differently.

Beyond the table is a large wooden door. There is a pentagram etched into the surface. You walk around

5 - Step Into Power

the table and stand facing the door. You raise your hand and trace the pentagram with your finger.

The door opens.

And here's where I'll leave you to explore...
(20 minutes)

When you feel ready, visualise the doorway that you came through and take yourself back there. Look back at where you've been and give thanks to those who helped you on your journey.

Go through the door and walk around the stone table. Walk back out through the tunnel and keep walking through all its twists and turns. You soon find yourself back at your starting point.

Slowly allow this image to fade. You find yourself standing in your sacred space once again.

Follow the instructions in appendix 2 to finish.

At the end of your journeys, spend time writing or painting about your experiences. It is always fun to look back at where you've come from and to see your progress.

6

Step Into The Boundless

Cosmic Magick – As Above, So Below

The practice offered in this book has taken you through a process aimed at helping you to unify with energies beyond yourself. By focusing on something, by studying it, and by knowing it on every level, you become unified with it. So far you have unified with your inner world, with your immediate environment, and with the vibrational world. You are now going to widen your awareness even further.

You will now be extending your experience out into the solar system. Once again, reminding yourself that you are a part of the great whole.

Throughout the world there are ancient temples, standing stones, sacred sites, and burial grounds placed in alignment with the Sun, the Moon, and other planets and stars. The planets were seen as powerful bodies and to some of our ancestors they represented gods and goddesses. However, since the rise of the monotheist God and the rejection by monotheist religion of the worship of any other gods/goddesses, reverence for these cosmic bodies has faded.

For many people now, apart from the difference between day and night, and the reading of daily columns in tabloids or magazines with some humour and a little suspicion, there is very little awareness of their movements or influence.

For thousands of years pre-monotheism astrology was not only a mathematical and mythical study but it was also a living practice – one which involved the whole community in celebration and ritual. Intuitively-based personal exploration of planetary influence is a lost art and it is difficult to make sense of it through present-day popular astrology, as much of this is based on superstition and assumption.

This chapter will rekindle your ancient wisdom by reintroducing you to the planets and the solar system from an experiential point of view. This will allow you to develop understanding of their influence from a personal perspective, and it will enable you to unify with the spiral dance of the cosmos.

Day and Night

Certain effects of the Sun and the Moon are obvious. For example, when the Sun is high in the sky we can feel its heat, and when the Moon is full its light gives everything a silvery glow. However there are other effects that aren't so immediately obvious. Throughout each month there is a dance of the Earth around the Sun, and the Moon around the Earth. This dance, through the laws of motion and gravity, influences the tides in the oceans. It also influences the gases in the upper atmosphere giving rise to changes in the Earth's magnetic fields.

Many life-forms, including humans, show behaviours that correspond to the changes in the relationships with these three planetary bodies. Practicing the following meditations and rituals at the appropriate times will bring these influences into awareness. You will come to understand your direct physical connection with nature and the immediate cosmos. You may be amazed at how your perception changes as you reaffirm links between the Sun, the Moon, and yourself.

The Moon

The Moon is our closest planetary body. It has an intimate relationship with the Earth and indeed with all of the life upon it. As the Moon circles the Earth the waters are drawn out towards it. Every water-dwelling creature must be aware of the huge changes that occur. There are many examples of marine life timing their breeding and behaviour cycles with those of the Moon. The Moon seems to effect human cycles also. The average length of the human female cycle of ovulation is almost identical to the period between the two full Moons. In many studies it has been shown that all humans have cyclic patterns of behaviour that change according to the Moon – from increasing birth rates to varying levels of 'lunacy' and crime. Perhaps, since humans have begun to live indoors and rely on electric lights, we are now less aware of the effects of the Moon. The following practice will reawaken your awareness.

Moon Bathing

Before you start the magickal Moon work, become familiar with the sensation of Moonlight.

> *At full Moon lie down on the ground and experience the light. Look at the colours around you and notice what happens to them when the Moon is at its brightest. Feel the Moon energy. Feel the light on your skin. Notice how you experience it.*
>
> *Do you have any unusual sensations? Can you feel the light enter you?*
>
> *Look at the Moon. What do you notice? What do you see?*
>
> *Close your eyes, what do you feel?*
>
> *Try howling. It has a wonderful effect.*

6 - Step Into The Boundless

Celebrate the Moon

You can explore your relationship with the Moon by making a point of looking out for it every night.

> *Keep a Moon journal and note down the phases of the Moon. You may want to draw or paint it as it changes shape or colour depending on the weather and the phase. You could photograph it or look at it through a telescope or binoculars. Get to know it, understand its changing shape, and the way the light of the Sun and the shadow of the Earth play upon it.*
>
> *Also in your journal write down your mood each day, your energy levels, and any physical changes you feel. Notice how things change as the Moon shifts through the waxing and waning cycle. Notice what happens to other people. You may see patterns here as well. If you have a menstrual cycle does it coincide with the phases of the Moon?*

Do this every day for at least a month. If you are interested in gaining more insight into your personal connection to Moon energy, I suggest you keep a Moon journal for four or five Moon cycles. This will give you an insight into any regular changes in behaviour, or in physical and emotional patterns.

Prayers to the Moon

During this time, every day for at least the first month, as you look up at the Moon, repeat the corresponding words below for each of the four phases. The Full Moon and the Dark/New Moon phases last three days each, and the rest of the time the Moon will be Waxing or Waning.

Full Moon
Great Moon, pulling the tides,
Magick mirror of silver light.
You peak and swell, the time of power.
Hail and welcome to the Night.

Waning Moon
Great Moon, pulling the tides,
Magick mirror of diminishing light.
You shrink and fade, the time of respite.
Hail and welcome to the Night.

Dark (New) Moon
Great Moon, pulling the tides,
Magick mirror of unseen light.
You cloak and hide, the time of shadows.
Hail and welcome to the Night.

Waxing Moon
Great Moon, pulling the tides,
Magick mirror bringing new light.
You expand and refresh, the time of growth.
Hail and welcome to the Night.

Astral Journey to the Moon
30 minutes

The Moon is generally associated with the unconscious, the dream world, and psychic and intuitive ability. When you journey to the Moon you will not only be exploring the energy of the Moon itself but you will also be exploring your deep psyche – the part of you that is generally hidden from consciousness. The Moon is also traditionally a symbol of your unconscious drives, your emotions, and your intuitive ability.

Follow instructions in appendix 1.

Slowly allow the image of the room to fade. You find yourself surrounded by a blue-white light. Looking above, you can see endless darkness dotted with millions of stars. Beneath your feet you can see dry white rocks and sand. In the distance there are hills, deep crevices, and craters. You feel light and free. At first you can hear no sound at all.

As you listen more carefully you slowly become aware of choral voices. They are soft and light. You listen more intently. You become aware of another sound, a deeper sound, a slow, rhythmical, vibrating base note that fades in and out.

You begin to walk forwards. Your movement feels effortless and you find yourself leaving the ground slightly with each step. There is no wind and your footprints remain in the white sand without any disturbance.

Ahead of you is a deep black crater with raised edges. You begin to walk towards it. As you near the crater you notice how black the shadow is compared to the brightness of the outer lunar landscape. The seemingly endless shadow intrigues you and you make your way to the edge.

This is where I leave you to explore… (20 minutes)

When the time is up, finish what you are doing and bring yourself back to the edge of the crater. Turn away and walk back the way you came stepping in the footprints that you made on your way here. When you arrive at your starting point, give thanks and slowly allow the image to fade.

Follow instructions in appendix 2.

Take a moment to recall your journey. When you are ready, write it down, and/or draw pictures if you like. Remember to write how you felt, and describe images, events, and any conversations you may have had with other beings or animals.

6 - Step Into The Boundless

The Sun

Due to large corporations having a vested interest in our use of skin cream and sunglasses, the Sun has become a symbol of fear. The aggressive and deceitful marketing of products, that include ever increasing 'SPF' and 'EPF' factors, mean that we rarely get to see the natural light of the Sun or feel the true healing effects on our skin. People have been taught to be suspicious of their own body's response, and instead they rely on questionable chemical concoctions to 'protect' them. People who wear sunglasses are losing out on the wonderful healing properties that the light of the Sun has on their eyes. However, before this the Sun was seen as a bringer of health, vitality, and happiness. Its healing properties were recognised as an essential element of life. Every morning when the Sun rose up over the horizon it would have been a cause for celebration.

Sun Bathing

Sun bathing is a beautiful, sensual, and healing experience. If you remain conscious of your personal tolerance of the sunlight you can listen to the messages from your skin and come out of the Sun when your body has had enough. The time will vary according to the place, time, and season.

> *For this exercise, simply spend some time consciously experiencing the light of the Sun. Lie down in the sunlight, preferably naked, and feel its affect on you. Be aware of the affect on your skin, your breath, and your internal organs. Feel the different sensations of the heat and the light.*

Prayers to the Sun

These affirmations will help you feel more connected to the turning of the Earth and the rising and the setting of the Sun. You will come to know how you are affected by the changes. You will develop an intimate relationship between your body and the vast cosmic bodies of the Earth and the Sun. You will connect deeply with the rhythms of our solar system.

At Dawn (or upon rising)

Turn to the East and raise your arms, palms upwards, and say:

Great life-giver rising in the East.
As the Earth turns,
you bring the light to wash away the darkness,
waking all to the songs of life,
shifting the moment to Morning.
Hail and welcome to the Dawn.

At Noon

Face the South and say:

Great life-giver highest in the South.
As the Earth turns,
you bring heat and light to nourish and heal,
lifting all to the power of joy and growth,
shifting the moment to Noon.
Hail and welcome to the Day.

6 - Step Into The Boundless

As the Sun Sets

Face the West and say:

Hail great life-giver falling into the West.
As the Earth turns,
you bring shimmering beauty to the skies,
moving all to watch and reflect,
shifting the moment to Evening.
Hail and welcome to the Dusk.

At Midnight (or just before sleeping)

Face the North and say:

Hail great life-giver hiding in the North.
As the Earth turns,
you give way to darkness, silence, and stillness,
allowing rest and regeneration,
shifting the moment to Night,
Hail and welcome to the Dark Skies.

Practice this every day for at least a month and you will understand its true and powerful effect.

You could do this during the same period that you are practicing the **Prayers to the Moon.**

Astral Journey to the Sun
30 minutes

When you journey to the Sun, you are not only connecting with the energy of this vast star, you are also symbolically connecting with the energy of your own life-force – your soul energy. There has always been a symbolic mystical connection between the Sun and the soul. In the Sun journey you have the opportunity to feel your full potential – the spark and the explosion of your personal power.

Follow instructions in appendix 1.

As the images of your room begin to fade, you find yourself flying high above the Sun. Below you can see the immense sphere of fire. There are powerful explosions of sound, colour, and movement, fast flowing rivers of white, yellow, orange, green, and blue, and fountains of heat and light raging towards you.

You become aware of searing heat as you begin to move closer. You are aware that your skin is beginning to melt, although you feel no pain. The closer you get to the Sun the more you feel yourself burning away into nothingness.

Soon you are no longer you. You have become part of this immense power. You are streaming, hot liquid; you are raging, rapid winds of gas and fire; you are mountains of explosive lava.

Here's where I'll leave you to explore… (20 minutes)

6 - Step Into The Boundless

When you are ready, finish what you are doing and give thanks. Move your consciousness away from the Sun. As you move away you find yourself becoming whole again. Look down at the Sun below you.

Slowly allow the images to fade.

Follow instructions in appendix 2.

Take a moment to recall your journey. Describe your experience, write it down or draw pictures if you like.

Awakening to Seasonal Shifts

In the year that it takes for our Earth to make its journey around the Sun we experience changes according to the seasonal shifts, not only in the external world but also within us. Like many other living beings on this planet we are affected by changes in the weather, the light, the heat, the radiation, and the magnetic shifts. They influence us on many levels.

Ancient astrologers looked up into the star-filled sky and found astrological points in the patterns of the stars and planets that corresponded with the seasonal shifts. The most obvious shifts are the summer and winter solstices – the longest and the shortest days of the year. These mark the middle of summer and the middle of winter. The equinoxes mark the middle of spring and autumn, where the days and nights are of equal length. The cross-quarter festivals, as they are known, are often called by the old English/Pagan names of: Imbolc, Beltane, Lammas, and Samhain, and they signal the beginning of each season.

Pre-Christian people would engage in festivals during each of these eight points of the year. The celebrations were reminders to prepare for the new season and to be grateful for the last. Without electric lights and heating, and without the ease of imported fruit and vegetables, as the seasons shifted, work, life, and activities had to change also. People not only recognised the changing seasons in nature, but they also recognised how this yearly cycle affected them on a personal level.

The Wheel of the Year
Northern Hemisphere

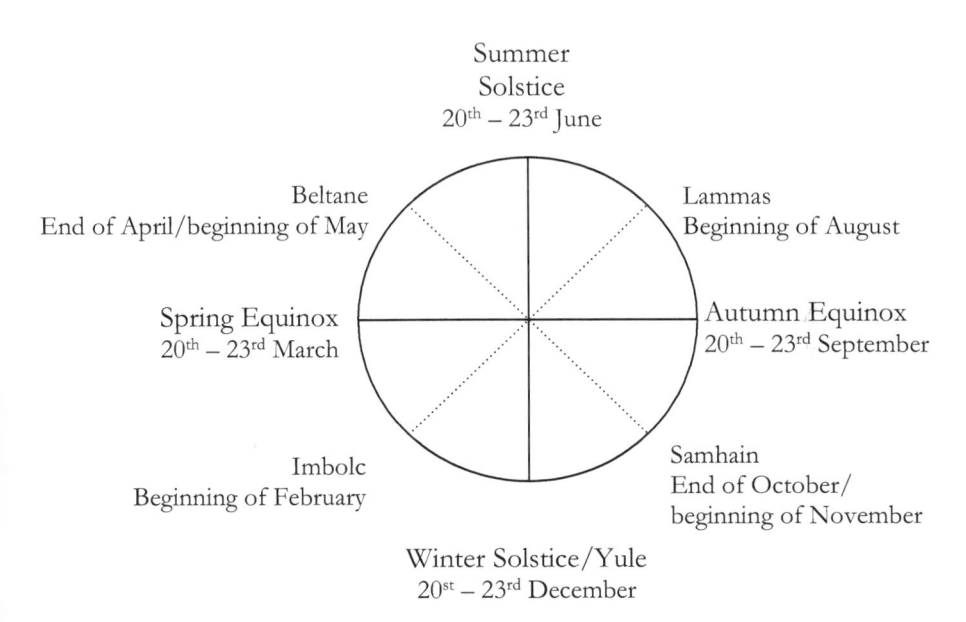

```
                    Summer
                    Solstice
                 20th – 23rd June

    Beltane                          Lammas
End of April/beginning of May    Beginning of August


  Spring Equinox                    Autumn Equinox
  20th – 23rd March                 20th – 23rd September


        Imbolc                       Samhain
  Beginning of February           End of October/
                                  beginning of November

              Winter Solstice/Yule
               20st – 23rd December
```

Note: In the southern hemisphere the dates are opposite to these, e.g. the dates for the summer solstice are exchanged with those of the winter solstice etc.

Monotheist religions co-opted ancient festivals and these were absorbed into the practices of the church. Many people now think of them as Christian celebrations. For example, the time of year that we now think of as Christmas stems from the ancient celebrations of the Winter Solstice. Long before Christianity was around it was celebrated as the time when the 'sun was reborn'. From this day onwards until the Summer Solstice the days become longer and lighter. It is clear to see why this was a cause for celebration.

Celebrating these ancient festivals gives us the opportunity to reflect on, and reminds us of, and the cycle of life, death, and rebirth that recurs year after year. This is reflected in the cycle of the cosmos, in all of the nature around us, and in ourselves. By working magickally with these festivals it is possible to recognise how these changes affect you on a physical, spiritual, and emotional level, and how you are so very connected with these universal shifts. Taking note of the seasonal movements reminds us that the Earth turns and circles through the cosmos, and that we are flying, and turning, and spinning through the cosmos with it.

Starting with the one nearest to your current season, aim to practice all eight of these rituals during the year (or even for many years). The effects of recognising these changes are very powerful. Whenever possible, perform these rituals outside to give you a real physical sense of the seasonal shifts. You could also add poems, songs, dances, or chants to these rituals if you choose.

Place on your altar items that represent the seasons. Find or write some appropriate music and dance to it during the ritual. Find out about traditions for each of the festivals and add these to the rituals too. Do whatever feels right to enhance your bodily understanding of the seasonal shifts. Also these rituals in particular are great to share with others.

6 - Step Into The Boundless

Align with Winter Solstice – Awaken
20th – 23rd December

In the middle of a long, cold, and dark winter, just when we feel it might continue forever, the Winter Solstice reminds us that the days will soon begin to lengthen, as the Sun is gradually climbs higher in the sky each day. The Sun is reborn and spring is just around the corner. At Yule you can celebrate the enchantment of the winter, the beauty that comes with the icy nights, and the excitement of freshly fallen snow.

Follow instructions in appendix 1.

State your intention: *"Tonight I will go within to find my inner light."*

Journey
When you are ready, light a white or gold candle and begin to look into the flame. At first, notice the darkness around it. Feel this darkness envelop you, and enter it fully. Fall into it. Notice what is in there and how it feels. Be in the darkness for a while feeling it around you, and be aware of the emptiness and the nothingness in your space. Spend some time exploring this moment. Connect with your feelings and sensations.

Now begin to notice the light of the flame piercing the darkness. Let it grow in your awareness. Feel the light envelop you and enter it fully. Fall into it. Now allow a feeling of expectation and wait. Begin to notice a tiny glimmer of light within your body. The bigger this inner light becomes the more any darkness within you is

I Am God

pushed aside. Begin to feel this light warming you. Watch as it burns brighter and brighter. Allow the light to fill you as it grows. Notice your sensations. Smile. What are you feeling?

Now allow your inner light to grow bigger and bigger, until it joins the external light, and allow yourself to expand into it. Feel a sense of joy as the light increases. Allow it to fill your being. Allow images to come.

Contemplate
What does this time of year mean to you? Do you have memories? Does it inspire something in you? Meditate on this for a while.

Speak and Dance
Now stand up in your circle. Pick up the candle and hold it above you. Breathe the light. Let words come, and speak these words out loud. When you have finished replace the candle.

Exaggerate the feeling of this light within your body. Allow any sounds and movement to come. Allow the light to inspire you to move or chant. If your body needs to express something let this happen.

Follow instructions in appendix 2.

Over the next few weeks keep hold of this sense of growing light and growing life. Notice the length of the days, the movement through the winter and towards the spring, and notice the changes that happen in your body.

6 - Step Into The Boundless

Align with Imbolc – Inspire
Beginning of February

As the Sun moves ever higher in the sky, the land becomes warmer which initiates the beginnings of spring. Imbolc comes from an old Celtic word meaning 'ewe's' milk' or 'in the womb'. This suggests an idea of things being almost ready to materialise. Traditionally candles or fires are used in this festival to represent the growing power of the Sun and the increasing light, hence the co-opted Christian 'Candlemas'.

Follow instructions in appendix 1.

State your intention: *"Tonight I will revitalise and connect with my light-filled power."*

Journey
As the images begin to fade you find yourself inside a cave. You can feel the cold stone beneath you.

There is no daylight here but, even so, the stone around you has a gentle yellow glow giving you a feeling of warmth, and a little light to see the inner walls of the cave. Breathe deeply into the space and feel the energy of the Earth here.

Begin to visualise yourself as a snake coiled up against the ground. The snake begins to stretch as if from a long winter sleep. As you connect with this Earth-snake, notice the sensation of this serpent energy at the base of your spine. Breathe deeply and watch yourself as the Earth-snake begins to uncoil, rising up and pushing through the earth above. Allow your physical body to reflect the snake's movements. Allow your sexual energy to ignite and sparkle with power as your body begins to vibrate. Continue to push up through the Earth until you break through and out into the daylight above. Feel yourself as the snake touching both the light and the deep dark inner Earth.

Experience the feeling of stretching and growing as you emerge from the cool darkness into the warmth of daylight. Experience the difference between these two worlds. Allow this feeling to fill your being. Allow images to come.

Contemplate
Light a candle and look into the flame. What does the growing light mean? What does this time of year represent for you? Does it inspire something in you? Do you have memories of early spring? Meditate on this for a while.

Speak and Dance
Next, stand up and allow any words, sounds, and movement to come. If your body needs to express something, let this happen. Dance your Imbolc dance.

Follow instructions in appendix 2.

This is a great time of year to spring-clean your house. Clear out anything that is gathering dust, and anything you don't use. Pay particular attention to the corners. Clear them of clutter and clean them thoroughly, making space for new growth.

Align with Spring Equinox – Nurture
20th - 23rd March

This celebration marks the middle of spring. The days and nights are now of equal length. At this point in the year you may begin to notice that everything is coming alive and everything is awakening. You may feel the spark of the life-force as it magickally breathes into everything. Roots, buds, shoots, and seeds are feeling the radiating warmth and beginning to burst into growth. We now need to energise the snake ready for action. It's time to hatch the cosmic egg! For this ritual, find a small polished stone. Choose one that attracts you and hold it in your hand throughout the ritual.

Follow instructions in appendix 1.

State your intention: *"In the coming season I will nurture my new growth."*

Journey
Sit down and place the stone in the palm of your hand. Look into the stone and slowly close your eyes. As you do this, hold the image of the stone in your mind. This is your 'cosmic egg'. As you watch your cosmic egg it begins to grow. Visualise placing it down in front of you, and watch as it expands large enough for you to climb inside.

Once you are inside, begin to explore. What images do you see inside it? Just like the spring manifests new growth, your egg can show you what is ready and waiting to grow and manifest in your life. Allow the cosmic egg to take you where it wants you to go, and to show you what you need to know. Watch as you are given information about this next phase in your life. What does the cosmic egg tell you about the steps that you need to take in order for things to manifest most usefully?

Contemplate
What does this time of year represent for you? Does it inspire something in you? Do you have memories of springtime? What seeds can you plant for the next phase? Meditate on this for a while.

Speak and Dance
While holding the images and feelings in your mind and body, allow any sounds, words, or movement to come. If your body needs to express something let this happen. Awaken to a springtime dance. Let your body experience the universal life-force expanding within you.

Follow instructions in appendix 2.

Your cosmic egg is now filled with the energy necessary to move into the next phase of your life. At the next opportunity release the cosmic egg back into nature. You could plant it in the Earth or throw it in the sea or a river. Your dreams will awaken and will be released from the confines of the egg.

By freeing the symbol, you are allowing your mind to trust that the things it represents will come into fruition or 'hatch' into life.

6 - Step Into The Boundless

Align with Beltane – Create
End of April/beginning of May

Beltane marks the very beginnings of summer. The Earth is in a powerful phase of growth, and everything is bathed in green. The focus of Beltane is the fertile land creating new life. Now it's time to celebrate and revere the wildness of our sacred sexuality. The traditional weaving maypole dances of Mayday are a reflection of this.

Follow instructions in appendix 1 and find some music that fills you with passion.

State your intention: *"I open my heart and body to meet my sexual potency."*

Repeat the chant:
*"I am my body. I am the Earth.
I fire my passion. I power my birth."*

Journey
Put on the music and, as you chant, focus on your pelvic area and allow your breath to reach deeply into this place. As you begin to find a rhythm in your breathing and your chant, bend your knees and allow your hips to follow the breath. As you inhale, relax the stomach muscles and tip the pelvis backwards allowing your buttocks to stick out. As you exhale, curl your pelvis up as your stomach and pelvic floor muscles tighten. Continue with this rhythm for a while. Now allow your hips to move from side to side and then to circle. Stay conscious of your breath as you explore the movements of your hips. Feel the fire and let the

wildness in. Feel a sense of your potent sexuality and the strength and power this brings.

When you feel that the energy is raised, sit down and notice the physical sensations and feelings that your body is experiencing. Experience yourself as a potent ball of passionate and creative energy. You are beautiful and dynamic. Allow this sensation to fill your being. Allow images to come. Look into your future and watch yourself expressing this energy freely and without apology.

Contemplate
What does this time of year mean to you? Does it inspire something in you? Do you have memories of early summer? Meditate on this for a while.

Speak and Dance
Stand up and allow any words, sounds and movement to come. Sing a sensual song of love and erotic power. Dance an arousing belly dance. It may be that there is a further rising of your sexual energy. Whatever is true for you in the moment let it happen.

Follow instructions in appendix 2.

Over the next few weeks remain with the Beltane energy. Use it to help you create – paint, dance, or sing. Make love with passion and abandon, go for walks in nature, and begin the creative project that you have been putting off.

Align with Summer Solstice – Thrive
20th – 23nd June

Now the summer is at its peak and so is everything else in nature. The days are longest at this time of year, the leaves are deep green on the trees, and the flowers are in full bloom. Feel the active solar energy as the Sun warms and nurtures you. Like the Sun, we are at our most powerful during this time of year. After the Summer Solstice the days will become shorter.

The following ritual will allow you to celebrate the abundance of energy in nature and in yourself. If you can, find a sunny place outdoors to perform the ritual.

Follow instructions in appendix 1.

State your intention: *"I open my being to inner power."*

Journey
Stand in the centre of your circle. Focus on the energy of the Sun. Let it enter you, and feel its vibration within you. In this moment of silence, allow your breath to come deeper and stronger. Now, sit down somewhere where you can feel the warmth of the Sun. Put your hand on your solar plexus – the area between the rib cage and the navel, and the connecting point to your personal, powerful Sun energy.

Close your eyes and allow the heat and light of the Sun to caress you. Feel it soaking through your skin and entering your body. Become aware of the nurturing and healing that your body experiences when bathed in sunlight. Now visualise a swirling Sun at your solar plexus point. Feel a sense of your personal strength and power wash over you. Watch as the Sun image grows, and allow it to light up your internal world. Let it fill your mind, your heart, and your soul.

Imagine yourself as an achiever and a creator. SMILE. Feel gratitude for everything you have achieved in your life and particularly in the last few months. Now let the image grow even bigger, so the light that is YOU fills the Universe. Enjoy this connection. Allow it to fill your being. Allow images to come.

Contemplate
Who are you in your full power? What can you achieve? What does this time of year mean to you? What does it inspire in you? Do you have memories of midsummer? Meditate on this for a while

Speak and Dance
Now stand up and allow any sounds and movement to come. If your body needs to express something, let this happen. Dance your Sun dance. Sing your Sun song. Smile with your whole body.

Follow instructions in appendix 2.

Over the next few weeks embody this powerful light. Take it everywhere with you. Remind yourself of the creative power you felt during the ritual. Remind yourself of your achievements. Smile often.

Align with Lammas – Produce
Beginning of August

The Sun's waning phase is noticeable now, as the nights continue to become shorter. Although it is often the hottest time of the year, it signals the first steps into autumn, and at this time we too will begin our waning phase. The word Lammas comes from a Saxon word which means 'Loaf Mass'. It was traditionally a celebration of the harvest of the grain – the first harvest of the year. It is a time to remember the gifts that the Earth creates for us. It is particularly important to remember that the grain that is harvested at this time of year not only feeds us now but it also becomes the seeds for sowing next year... and so the cycle continues. We receive; we give back. If possible find a quiet place outside for this ritual.

Follow instructions in appendix 1.

State your intention: *"I give to the Earth in return."*

Journey
Sit down and allow yourself to feel held by the Earth. Now, either sitting or kneeling, put your forehead and hands to the Earth. Become aware of the Sun above you and the Earth beneath you. Imagine the Earth as a mother who nurtures, feeds, and supports you.

Visualise yourself being held by the mother, and create the sensation within you that the Earth is gently rocking you. Raise a feeling of gratitude for all of the abundance you experience in your life, and all the beautiful creations that have come from the seeds that you may have planted in the spring. Allow this sensation to fill your being. Allow images to come.

Contemplate
In this sacred moment, remember your experience of the last few months. Remember the seeds of ideas or projects that you planted during the early spring. What has come of them? Are they still underground? Have they started to grow? Or are they fully grown — flowering and bearing fruit? Are there any seeds that you planted that have turned out to be unhelpful? Why did you plant them? What made them unhelpful? Remember this information for the next time you plant seeds. What does this time of year mean to you? Does it inspire something in you? Meditate on this for a while.

Speak and Dance
Stand up and allow any sounds and/or movement to come. If your body needs to express something, let this happen. What is your dance and song of abundance?

Follow the instructions in appendix 2.

Over the next few weeks take real notice of the food you eat, particularly vegetables and grains. Attempt to raise in yourself a feeling of gratitude to the Earth for its abundance and nurturing ability.

Align with Autumn Equinox – Gather
20th - 23rd September

At this time of year the day and night are in perfect equal balance. The power of the Sun is continuing to wane. It is now the middle of autumn. The nights begin to get longer, and the leaves are changing colour and falling from the trees. This time of year is also known as the Harvest Festival as now the last of the fruits and vegetables are gathered in. We are reminded that winter is not far away and we must prepare for the colder times ahead. Having been active during the peak of summer, it's time to begin to gather in our gifts, to bring our focus inward, and to give ourselves time and space to rest and regenerate. We too will enter our waning phase and will use the autumn and winter months for resting and recharging our batteries.

Follow the instructions in appendix 1.

State your intention: *"I give time to myself to heal and recharge."*

Journey
Sit down in your circle and place your hands on the Earth. Visualise roots growing down through your hands and fingers and reaching into the Earth's core. Become aware of a deep dark world within you and allow this space to open up. As you connect with the Earth's energy, allow it to flow into all these spaces. Feel the calm this brings. Like the roots of the trees and plants during this time of year, we can stretch into the abundant Earth and draw our nutrients from deep

within. Visualise your roots reaching deeper and deeper, and love the Earth.

Allow your breath to come deeper. Gently allow sounds out with each exhale. Repeat this exhaled sound until it becomes a resonating vibration in your body. Continue to visualise your roots reaching deep into the Earth as you vibrate this sound. Feel the vibration moving though your flesh, your bones, and your internal organs. Visualise every cell being cleansed and nourished by this. Have the sense also that you are releasing all the stress and tension that you may have been carrying through the more active seasons. Allow this releasing sound to continue until you feel that the work is done and that you are now clear of tension and fully able to rest.

Contemplate
What does this time of year mean to you? Does it inspire something in you? Do you have memories of the autumn? Meditate on this for a while.

Speak and Dance
Stand up and allow any further sounds, words, and/or movement to come. Let your body express what it needs. What is your dance and song of harvest?

Follow the instructions in appendix 2.

Over the next few weeks, if you feel any stress or tension, allow time for yourself to breathe and vibrate. Use it to clear away any leftover stress that you don't need, and use it to remind you to give time and quiet space to yourself.

Align with Samhain – Release
End of October, beginning of November

Traditionally Samhain marks the end of the old year and the beginning of the new. It is also the time when the veil between the worlds of the living and the dead becomes thin, giving us the opportunity to reflect on death and loss, and to remember and honour our ancestors. Darkness and death are not to be feared, but are to be revered as an important part of the cycle of life, death, and rebirth. Without the death of the old there is no space for new growth and regeneration. The falling leaves of the early winter remind us to release the old and unnecessary growth in order to make way for the new. It is a time to clear the cobwebs of the past and let go of unhelpful or destructive elements in our lives.

You will need: *A dark veil and some items that symbolically represent things you would like to let go of – an unhelpful habit, a need, a relationship, or an addiction, for example.*

Follow instructions in appendix 1.

State your intention: *"I will end and begin, and end and begin."*

Journey
Put the veil over your head and visualise yourself walking in darkness for a while. Where will you go? What will you find? When you are ready, lay the veil on the floor in front of you. Place the first symbolic object on the veil. As you do, visualise your life free of

the things your symbol represents. Breathe deeply and inhale the positive feelings as you watch yourself release these things. Visualise this thing shrinking and fading away like the leaves falling from the trees. When you feel ready, say out loud, 'I release you... (insert a word that represents your thing)'. Repeat this exercise until you have released all of your chosen things. Then fold the veil over all the items that symbolise them so they can no longer be seen.

Contemplate
Next, allow your mind to focus, with love, on those who are no longer walking in this world. Remember their details, the clothes they wore, their smell, and some of the moments that you shared. Sit in silence, smile, and vibrate the feeling of love. Feel calm and safe in their presence. Now, consider, what does this time of year mean to you? What does it inspire? Meditate on all this for a while.

Speak and Dance
Take some time in the darkness to reflect on your own mortality. Stand up and open to the sensation of letting go, of release, of death, and let it fill your being. Allow any sounds, words, images, and/or movement to come. If your body needs to express something, let this happen. What is your dance of death and rebirth?

Follow the instructions in appendix 2.

Over the next few weeks dispose of the items you wrapped in the cloth, with a sense of relief. Do this safely and with care for the environment.

6 - Step Into The Boundless

Planetary Power

In ancient spiritual philosophy it is understood that we are influenced by the planets both physically and emotionally. Over thousands of years each of the planets were given attributes based on the myths of the times and also on their movements through the cosmos. These myths and attributes have continued over the years, and the symbolic associations of the planets are now very powerful within the collective psyche. There are a variety of common colour attributes for the planets. I prefer the correspondences used in the Qabalistic Tree of Life, and I have used these in the following rituals.

The attributes of each planet represent a particular universal energy and a particular aspect of consciousness. Working with the planetary vibrations enables you to find out for yourself the effects of the planets, and also to explore the aspect of yourself that the planet symbolically represents. It enables you to experience familiar and unfamiliar energies that are all equally valuable and that are all a part of who you are.

In order for you to become whole, everything about you must be integrated and accepted, even the parts that you don't like or want. If you give your consciousness new and different experiences it can enable you to be free from your past limitations, and therefore you can heal in a profound way. The mind cannot tell the difference between 'real' or 'imagined' experience. Therefore, the following rituals can give your psyche opportunities to grow in ways that were previously unimaginable.

7 Planetary Rituals

Each of the following rituals involves speaking words out loud. This calls the energy associated with the planet into the space and brings the vibration into your body. Once you have located the feeling in your body, begin to visualise the planetary symbol. Focus on the image at your 'third eye' point – slightly above your eyebrows in the centre of your forehead. Hold the image there for as long as you can. If you lose it, keep bringing it back.

You will be also asked to 'intone' the vibration of this energy. Your body is surrounded by sound and other vibrations constantly. Intoning is a useful way of balancing and aligning with these vibrations. When making a long hum or 'ahhh' sound in your body you will feel physical vibrations moving through you. Intoning can have a deeply healing effect. It is an internal 'energy' massage. It can sometimes feel as if everything is being moved into place and that you are coming into alignment with the particular energy you are evoking.

As you feel the energy of the planet, and visualise the associated colour and symbol, allow this to inform the pitch of the sound that you make. Let this be intuitive. Don't try to prescribe it. Allow yourself to express whatever comes up for you. Different pitches will produce different vibrations in your body. Notice the areas of your body that are affected. You may feel tingling or you may see patterns or shapes. Depending on where you place your tongue in your mouth you may also hear some 'overtones'. These are high-pitched whistling sounds that can be heard alongside the sound you are making with

6 - Step Into The Boundless

your mouth. These bring even more powerful and healing vibrations into your body.

Allow the energy of the planet to really move through your body. Notice how each planetary energy is experienced differently. Notice what image this calls up for you. Does it resonate with a particular aspect of your personality? Do you like this part of yourself? Can you integrate it and love it? Wait and watch. Allow the visualisations to come. Experience them in your body as well as in your mind. They may bring shapes or patterns, they may become visual journeys, or they may bring memories. You may be inspired to move your body or to make more sounds. Go with the inspiration and come to know the different planetary powers.

To begin each ritual follow the instructions in appendix 1 and to finish each ritual follow the instructions in appendix 2. Take time to recall your experience and record it in your journal.

When you have explored these rituals once or twice and have understood the power and energy of each planet, you can use them to bring these energies into your life. If you need to create some boundaries in a situation, for example, you can use the Mars meditation for this purpose. These rituals are a very powerful and instantaneous way of inviting specific energies and feelings into your body and into your life.

Mercury
20 minutes

Associated Colour – Orange

When you work with the energies associated with the planet Mercury you are connecting with the part of your psyche that deals with the intellect – the ability to communicate rationally, to study, and to create formulas, charts, and equations. It helps you to resonate with the universal power of mathematical and scientific understanding, and the beauty of patterns and structure in nature, in design, and in thought.

Say:

"Messenger,
invite me into wisdom,
show me my truth.
The art of science,
the beauty of mathematics.
Open me to my knowledge."

Pause to invoke the energies into your body....
Allow a humming sound to emerge from deep within you. This is your planetary sound for Mercury. Intone this vibration until you feel that it is a part of you. Visualise the glowing orange planetary symbol at your brow point and say:

"Mercury, show me your power"

Watch, wait, and explore...

6 - Step Into The Boundless

Venus
20 minutes

Associated Colour – Green

The planet Venus is associated with the energy of love, trust, openness, play, and creative and sexual freedom. It is nurturing and sensual. When this power enters you, you will be opening yourself to the playful and free-flowing pleasures of your body and mind. Often these aspects of ourselves are disallowed. Maybe here you will allow yourself to enjoy and play with these energies.

Say:

*"Beauty,
invite me into wisdom.
Show me my truth,
the joy of play,
the wonder of love.
Open me to my knowledge"*

Pause to invoke the energies and feelings into your body... Allow a humming sound to emerge from deep within you. This is your planetary sound for Venus. Intone this vibration until you feel that it is a part of you. Visualise the glowing green planetary symbol at your brow point and say:

"Venus, show me your power"

Watch, wait, and explore...

Mars
20 minutes

Associated Colour – Red

Mars energy relates to directive, and forward moving energy. It helps us recognise, hold, and/or push through restriction and boundaries. It connects with the aspect of your psyche that deals with rules and regulations. This is the energy that helps you to be clear with your own boundaries. It helps you to say 'no', and to stand up for what you believe to be right. It helps you to decide and divide. It thrusts you forward with focus and drive.

Say:

> *"Warrior,*
> *invite me into wisdom,*
> *show me my truth.*
> *The drive of righteousness,*
> *the courage of honest expression.*
> *Open me to my knowledge"*

Pause to invoke the energies and feelings into your body.... Allow a humming sound to emerge from deep within you. This is your planetary sound for Mars. Intone this vibration until you feel that it is a part of you. Visualise the glowing red planetary symbol at your brow point and say:

"Mars, show me your power"

Watch, wait and explore...

Jupiter
20 minutes

Associated Colour – Blue

The energy associated with Jupiter is that of expansive abundance. It is extravagant and excessive. When you work with this energy you are resonating with the area of your psyche that is optimistic, giving, and loving. It is also associated with philosophy, free-thinking, and open-mindedness and it is with this energy that you explore the deeper principles of life. Here you are benevolent and philanthropic. Here you expand by giving.

Say:

> *"Healer,*
> *Invite me into wisdom.*
> *Show me my truth,*
> *the abundance of love,*
> *the freedom of giving.*
> *Open me to my knowledge"*

Pause to invoke the energies and feelings into your body... Allow a humming sound to emerge from deep within you. This is your planetary sound for Jupiter. Intone this vibration until you feel that it is a part of you. Then visualise the glowing blue planetary symbol at your brow point and say:

"Jupiter, show me your power"

Watch, wait and explore...

Saturn
20 minutes

Associated Colour – Absence of Colour/Black

The energy associated with Saturn relates to, limitation, and self-discipline, the laws of life and nature, and the cyclical patterns of death and rebirth. It can give us strength to make necessary change in our lives. When we resonate with this energy, we are entering the area of our psyche that deals with endings, with loss, with the structure of time, and with our experience of judicial, natural, and cosmic law.

Say:

> *"Teacher,*
> *invite me into wisdom.*
> *Show me my truth,*
> *the transformation of death,*
> *the supremacy of law*
> *Open me to my knowledge"*

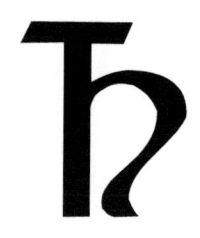

Pause to invoke the energies and feelings into your body... Allow a humming sound to emerge from deep within you. This is your planetary sound for Saturn. Intone this vibration until you feel that it is a part of you. Then visualise the glowing black planetary symbol at your brow point and say:

"Jupiter, show me your power"

Watch, wait and explore...

6 - Step Into The Boundless

Uranus
20 minutes

Associated Colour – All colour/white

The energies associated with Uranus are: the unexpected, revolution, change, and freedom of spirit. With Uranus you are connecting with the area in your psyche that is independent – the eccentric part of you that disregards the rules, has free will, and is guided by intuition and personal genius. When you resonate with Uranus energy you will feel free to shine your own light without apology, and to be true to yourself regardless of the judgements of others.

Say:

> *"Knower,*
> *invite me into wisdom.*
> *Show me my truth,*
> *the sovereignty of freedom,*
> *the genius of intuition.*
> *Open me to my knowledge."*

Pause to invoke the energies and feelings into your body... Allow a humming sound to emerge from deep within you. This is your planetary sound for Uranus. Intone this vibration until you feel that it is a part of you. Then visualise the glowing rainbow-coloured planetary symbol at your brow point and say:

"Uranus, show me your power"

Watch, wait and explore...

Neptune
20 minutes

Associated Colour – Infinite sparkling rainbow light

The energies associated with Neptune are inspiration, enlightenment, and intuition. When you resonate with Neptune you are connecting with the mystical beginnings of time, of life, and of everything. It is the spark before manifestation. When we know creatrix, we know all. Through personal evolution we meet ourselves in love. In this we can truly open to a love for all.

Say:

> *"Creator,*
> *invite me into wisdom.*
> *Show me my truth,*
> *the fountain of divine light,*
> *the doorway to Union.*
> *Open me to my knowledge"*

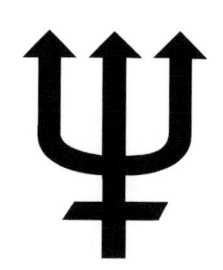

Pause to invoke the energies and feelings into your body... Allow a humming sound to emerge from deep within you. This is your planetary sound for Neptune. Intone this vibration until you feel that it is a part of you. Then visualise the glowing sparkling planetary symbol at your brow point and say:

"Neptune, show me your power"

Watch, wait and explore...

Pluto
20 minutes

Associated Colour – Silver

The energies associated with Pluto are personal transformation, the shadow, and ego death – releasing all that is false in you. This energy can be difficult and challenging. When you resonate with Pluto you have the opportunity to be the phoenix – re-birthing from the flames of ignorance and fear. When you know this power, you can be liberated through self-destruction – you will be Truth.

Say:

> *"Death,*
> *invite me into wisdom.*
> *Show me my truth,*
> *the transparency of honesty,*
> *the simplicity of authenticity.*
> *Open me to my knowledge."*

Pause to invoke the energies and feelings into your body... Allow a humming sound to emerge from deep within you. This is your planetary sound for Pluto. Intone this vibration until you feel that it is a part of you. Then visualise the glowing silver planetary symbol at your brow point and say:

"Pluto, show me your power"

Watch, wait and explore...

Travel to the Outer Cosmos
30 minutes

I prefer not to be too descriptive about this journey so I will give the instructions and, if you would like to explore what it brings, go ahead without expectation.

Go out for a walk with the intention of finding the stone that will take you on a journey to discover the cosmos. When you are near the correct stone it will call you to pick it up. Trust your intuition and bring your chosen stone home.

Follow the instructions in appendix 1.

When you are ready, hold the stone in the palm of your hand and ask it to show you the story of the universe. Allow the stone to melt into your palm and enter your body. Become the stone. Wait, watch, and experience this most profound journey.

When you have finished, ask the stone to bring you back to your current experience, and feel yourself fully back in your body and in your space. Use the breath to ground you and connect you.

Follow the instructions in appendix 2.

Recall and record your experience.

7

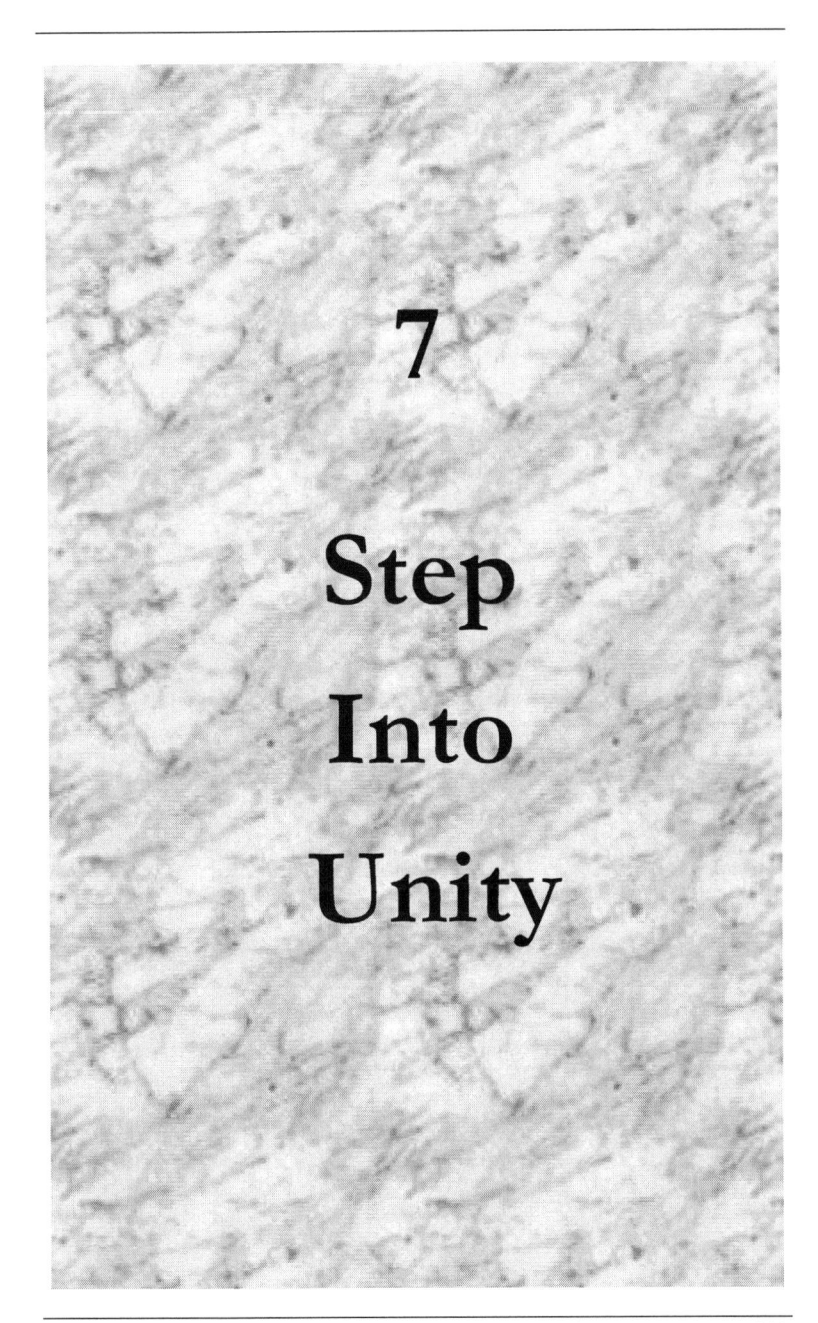

Step Into Unity

7 - Step Into Unity

Become the Divine Creator

In a monotheist driven culture we are given so much information about what we should or shouldn't be that many people don't know who they really are. We are constantly bombarded with images of the 'perfect' man, the 'perfect' woman, the 'perfect' family, the 'perfect' job, the 'perfect' spiritual person, and the 'perfect' home. People find that, instead of being happy with who they are and what they have, they constantly strive for something different. This creates feelings of frustration, stress, depression, and unhappiness.

*

Our value is currently measured by how precisely we can fit ourselves into defined boxes rather than how well we can express our own personal genius.

*

The work you have done so far in this book has been a process of freeing yourself from these moulds and finding the truth within in order to self-realise. The rituals and meditations in this chapter are extremely powerful and will enable you to finally become your divine self. You may have come across magickal work like this before but having come to this stage in this book, and after doing the work you have done so far, you may find that the experience now feels deeper, more profound, and more True.

Magickal Manifestation

When your Self has been realised as God you can do the will of the divine. As God you have the power to bring into being anything that you wish to create. As a divine being, in order to manifest, you simply need to create an intention, and then believe it down in the depths of your unconscious. The ritual below will help you do this.

Remember you were already divine before you began this process and everything you've done so far has hopefully helped you to see that. As a divine being you have already been creating your reality, but you were doing this unconsciously via 'little-you' and via your unhelpful beliefs. In order to create as a divine being the process is exactly the same except that now it is done with choice.

This may be difficult at first as you may not have fully shaken off the old patterns of belief about the nature of reality and creation. There are a few steps you will need to take in order to train your mind to bypass your disbelief and to have trust in your divine abilities. It is possible to learn this trust through practice. Eventually the tools presented below will become unnecessary. You will reach the point where all you need to do is to consciously speak, think, or believe something and it will become your reality.

In many early myth systems the cosmos, the Earth, and everything in existence is 'birthed' into being by a 'Great Mother'. These beliefs may have come from the witnessing of babies being born. Using conception and birth as a guide to manifestation makes the necessary steps of magick very obvious and straight-forward.

7 - Step Into Unity

	Conception and Birth	Steps	Manifestation Magick
1	Let's have a baby!	**Decide what you want.**	Be clear about your chosen creation.
2	Have cosmic sex.	**Bring the ingredients together in union.**	Raise your level of consciousness to an ecstatic state and become one with your chosen creation. Bring your being into alignment with it.
3	Conception	**Plant the seed.**	State your intention and use symbols to implant the belief into your unconsciousness.
4	Pregnancy	**Nurture the seed as it grows and matures.**	Establish the belief that it will eventually manifest.
5	Prepare for the new arrival.	**Be ready.**	Prepare your consciousness and your physical environment to make space for your creation to manifest.
6	Watch the body changing and growing.	**Look for evidence that your creation is on its way.**	Believe in the reality you choose rather than the reality that you perceive.
7	**Give birth**	**Manifestation**	**Receive**

The Use and Abuse of Magick

Magick is a practice in which the beliefs of a person are changed on a deep unconscious level in order to change their perception and therefore their environment. The changes are achieved through the use of:

- Symbolism
- Constant repetition
- Hypnotism
- Changing the level of consciousness – through ritual or other methods (music, lighting, mantra, rhythm, or incense etc.) – and flooding the unconscious with images, stories, and emotion.

These methods work directly with the unconscious in a language it understands. When symbols are implanted deep within a psyche which is already opened up by an altered state a **pathway of belief is forged**. Once it is put there it is very difficult to remove it. It is impossible to simply talk oneself out of a deeply-forged belief.

The methods have been used for thousands of years for many different reasons. Cultures and religions use them as a form of social control to brainwash or hypnotise people through coercion and indoctrination. Individuals have used them to gain personal power. Of course, anything can be used for harm or good depending on whose hands the knowledge falls into. This is why it is important to work on your personal development before beginning manifestation work. You are then more likely to be doing the work of your deeper Will rather than that of your ego or 'little-you'.

7 - Step Into Unity

Religions are still using the techniques, as are politicians, advertising agencies, and supermarkets, to name just a few. Most large corporations (I include religion here) use these techniques with the purpose of, knowingly and without apology, changing people's beliefs in order to manipulate them into buying their products. Every word, symbol, image, action, and ambient mood is placed with absolute care and with total knowledge of the effect it is likely to create. In the case of social control this brainwashing pervades our homes throughout our lives – from the fairy stories we are read as children to the TV programs, public 'health' warnings, 'news' papers, and magazines we come into contact with as adults. This is extremely disempowering. Your beliefs are being changed without your consent, minute by minute. However, you are now a magician in your own right. You are divine and you have no need to accept or believe. Personal magick is an ancient method of purposeful self-hypnosis. It uses exactly the same tools, but you get to choose the message.

The practice of magick can be used to manifest 'things'– a new car, a job, or a lover. A mystic also uses the tools of magick as a way to create a 'creator'. That is to lead themselves into union; to unite the 'Above' with the 'Below'; to join the microcosm with the macrocosm; to join the human consciousness with the great All; to become the divine in manifestation.

*

When you are the creator, every thought is an act of conscious manifestation.

*

Magickal Tools

There are many tools used in manifestation work:

- ❖ Visualisation
- ❖ Symbol formation
- ❖ Sound/dance/rhythm
- ❖ Mantra/chant
- ❖ Sacred geometry
- ❖ Repeated words and actions
- ❖ Meditation

The **ritual of the sacred circle** incorporates many of these elements. By repeating it, and using the carefully written words, actions, visualisations, shifts in consciousness, and symbols, you have been strengthening the unconscious belief that:

*

You are the centre of your universe and you are creating your own reality.

*

This first step that you have taken has been **absolutely necessary**, as without this belief none of the other methods will make a difference. Following is an example of manifestation magick that you can use for any conscious creation – bring love into your life, change a living arrangement, bring health, get a new car etc.

Magickal Methods

There are three stages to a successful manifestation ritual:

1. **Preparation**

    a. Know what you want
    b. Notice unconscious blocks to achieving your goal
    c. Create your intention sentence
    d. Create your talisman

2. **Create New Beliefs**

    a. Remind yourself that you are the creator
    b. Transform the consciousness
    c. Clear unhelpful beliefs
    d. Align with the chosen intention

3. **Trust and Release**

    a. Daily practice with your talisman
    b. Enhance feelings of gratitude
    c. Look for signs
    d. Forget

Using the above method you can create a ritual for any chosen purpose. The next section will guide you through the steps of creating your own manifestation ritual.

Magickal Manifestation Ritual

1. Preparation

   a. **Know what you want**

      Decide on something you would like to create. This could be a new thing, a new feeling, or a new experience for example. N.B. unless a person specifically asks you for help it is very important that all magick is focused around yourself and under no circumstances should you attempt to change someone else or affect their will, even if you think it is for their own good. In my experience it is a dangerous practice, both for you and for the other person involved. Instead ask what you can change about yourself in order to achieve the desired results. For example, if you want someone to fall in love with you create new beliefs about yourself so that you feel beautiful and desirable, rather than attempting to manipulate someone.

   b. **Notice unconscious blocks to achieving your goal**

      Make a list of all the unhelpful sentences and other things in your environment that are convincing you that this manifestation can't happen. For example: 'I don't have enough money', 'I'm not strong enough', 'my friends will disapprove', 'I don't look right', 'there isn't enough time'. This will be called your 'unhelpful list'. These thoughts must be brought to consciousness otherwise they will eat away at your new beliefs.

c. **Create your intention sentence**

Write a precise sentence which describes your intention. It must have only <u>one focus</u>. It must use the <u>present tense</u> and <u>positive language</u>. For example: "I have a great new job", "I have a loving partner", "I am enjoying my new car", or "I am healthy". **Not** "I want to get rid of my illness" or "I don't want to be unhappy anymore". Remember, the words you put out there are instilled with energy. Using words like 'unhappy' and 'illness' will align you with precisely what you don't want. This is why it is very important that you put <u>careful consideration</u> into this step.

d. **Create your talisman**

Magick uses symbols to bypass the intellect. Often, when you really want something, your mind will give you many 'logical' reasons why you can't have it, as you will have seen in your 'unhelpful sentence' list. So, in order to speak directly to the unconscious, you will need to use symbolic language. Having decided on your intention sentence, follow the instructions below.

- ❖ Start by writing down the first letter in each word of your sentence. Now, delete any repeated letters. 'I am happy at home' becomes I A H.
- ❖ Create a symbol using these letters by making a simple pattern or shape with them that appeals to you. It works better if you can't identify the individual letters in your final symbol as it is important that your thinking mind is not stimulated during the ritual (this would bring you back to beta mind vibration). Try merging the letters into a single shape.
- ❖ Draw your symbol using a colour which you feel aligns with your intention. Perhaps also incorporate a little symbolic picture of the thing and/or an appropriate planetary symbol (having done the meditations earlier, you will have a sense of the correct planet to empower your symbol with).
- ❖ Draw a circle around it.
- ❖ Cut it out. It should be about palm-sized.
- ❖ This is your talisman

2. **Create new beliefs**

   a. **Remind yourself that you are the creator**

   Perform the **ritual of the sacred circle** (appendix 1).

   b. **Transform the consciousness**

   Practice the **foundation breath meditation** (appendix 1).

7 - Step Into Unity

c. **Clear the unhelpful beliefs**

   It is important to clear these before your psyche is ready to accept the new beliefs. Within the circle, read through the 'unhelpful list' without paying it too much attention. Then scribble out the words, tear up the paper, and throw it away, and/or burn it. Close your eyes and visualise a vortex or cauldron in the centre of the circle and watch your unhelpful list, and all the words on it, disappear into a void. Sit for a while feeling a sense of empty readiness, and feeling that you are cleansed of the unhelpful thoughts. This may sound very simple but in your altered state it will have a profound effect.

d. **Align with chosen intention**

   ❖ Visualise yourself enjoying the experience of your chosen intention. Using the example above (I am happy at home) you would visualise yourself at home smiling and laughing with the people around you. Make the images big and colourful, and watch them glow with sparkling light. Exaggerate the emotions in your body by smiling and laughing. It is very important to FEEL.

   ❖ Repeat out loud your full **intention sentence** over and over again. Repeat it faster and faster until it no longer makes sense. At this point, chant it as a sound and syllable mantra, find the rhythm of it, and experience the sensations of this in your mind and body.

- ❖ As you continue with your mantra, begin to exaggerate the emotional experience of the visualisation even more – FEEL.
- ❖ Bring the emotions into your body by allowing some authentic movement to accentuate the rhythm of your mantra – use this body and sound rhythm for long enough to establish a shift in consciousness.
- ❖ At this stage you may choose to use erotic self-touch to BUILD THE ENERGY.
- ❖ Inhale the amazing emotions of your chosen intention, FEEL and SMILE (literally) – this is a very powerful action (as you know from the smile meditation) as it creates a physiological response.
- ❖ Fix a still picture of your intention in your mind. Hold it there for a while.
- ❖ Watch as this still picture now transforms into an image of the symbol that is on your talisman.
- ❖ Continue to repeat your (now meaningless) mantra in silence as you focus on the symbol. Hold the image of the talisman at your mid-brow point.
- ❖ Meditate on the talisman, exaggerating its colours, its size, and its intensity.
- ❖ Visualise the image rising up and away from your body and into the centre of the circle. Watch it growing in size and intensifying in colour.
- ❖ Take some faster and deeper breaths, then when you are at your energy peak, STOP! Hold your breath, and tense every muscle in your body. Watch your symbol explode in a cascade of rainbow light as it disperses out into the universe to do its work.

7 - Step Into Unity

- ❖ Exhale and relax your body. Give time to allow your body to express in any way that feels right.
- ❖ Relax for a while enjoying the feelings. Feel yourself breathing and safe inside your body. Feel the floor beneath you. Take some time to reflect.
- ❖ Follow instructions in appendix 2.

3. **Trust and release**

   a. **Daily practice with your talisman**

   Visualise the symbol every day for a week, and allow yourself to feel the appropriate emotions of your intention. This brings you into alignment with the energy you are asking for. Carry the talisman with you during this time, looking at it as often as you remember. Every time you do, allow yourself to feel the emotion of the intention.

   b. **Enhance feelings of gratitude**

   Prepare yourself to <u>receive</u> the changes. You must put yourself into a state of gratitude. Every day, for the next 10 days, either before you go to sleep or just after you wake up, write down, or speak out-loud, at least 20 things you feel grateful for, or meditate for 10 minutes on all the things you have and are happy about.

c. **Look for signs**

> Once you have created a belief deep inside your psyche it will lead you to your goal. Follow your intuition. If you feel an urge to take a different route, buy a particular magazine, or enter a competition, follow it. Look for signs of your intention arriving through the post, or notice the things that are changing around you as your environment begins to make way for your intention to manifest. Act, and see the world, as if the changes have happened already. Stay in touch with your intuition and follow the impulses.

d. **Forget**

> After 7 days, with a feeling of ceremony, either burn or bury the talisman in order to release it. This is an important step. You must let go of your conscious investment in the intention once it is buried deep in your psyche, so your unconscious can continue its work.

7 - Step Into Unity

Meet your Divine Self

Just like the thought-forms of the spirits of the Elements that you have already created, images of gods and goddesses can help you to understand your own inner divine self. Putting the experience of your personal divine outside of yourself by creating a thought form can be a useful tool to access the wisdom you hold within. When using thought-forms it is important to remember that they are self-created, but, at the same time, in order to get the most out of them, it is also important to generate a 'belief' in their 'reality'.

Monotheist religion has offered us a warped view of divinity: a collective thought-form of a bearded man in the clouds who judges, 'protects', or punishes us according to our behaviour. The concept of any female divine presence has practically disappeared, except in the form of the 'virgin' Mary – a desexualised image of the divine mother.

We are taught to accept only those aspects of ourselves that reflect the monotheist thought-forms. All aspects that are not reflective of these are deemed 'bad', 'wrong', 'unspiritual', or 'evil' – for example, the sexual, sensual, natural (hairy, bloody, smelly, juicy, birth-giving), fun, indulgent, romantic, playful, and hedonistic, aspects of ourselves. In older polytheistic religions the myth structure reflects the nature of humanity more holistically – there are gods and goddess of love, indulgence, fun, wine, and war etc.

The following journeys take you to meet the divine truth that is you in all your aspects. They will give you the opportunity to ask yourself questions and learn your truth. You can ask your divine being anything, and you will always receive an answer. Each one of the following journeys encompasses different aspects of yourself – the playful and childlike aspect, the sensual and experienced adult aspect, and the magickal and wise aspect. You will find that these divine beings accept everything that you already express of yourself, and they may even tempt you into exploring further into the experience of YOU than you have ever allowed.

For each of the following journeys, begin with the instructions in appendix 1 and end by following the instructions in appendix 2. In my description below I will use terms which describe the female gender. In your journeys please use a gender which you feel reflects you most closely. You may also wish to repeat the journeys and have the divine beings represent different genders for you – therefore reflecting even more aspects of yourself.

Child
30 minutes

Slowly allow any images of your room to fade. You find yourself standing in thick green grass. You can feel its lush softness under your bare feet. The grass is cool and wet with tiny drops of morning dew. You lift your eyes and look out onto a beautiful meadow. The Sun is rising over the horizon, and its warmth caresses your skin. There are small crops of colourful spring flowers dotted here and there, and you can hear the gentle bubbling of a small stream nearby. In the distance you can make out a large Oak tree. Its size suggests that it has been here for many years. You feel compelled to walk towards it.

As you pick your way through the tiny wild flowers, you take pleasure in the sensation of the soft grass underfoot. You continue to walk, taking in the beauty of this place and feeling the Sun's powerful energy warming you. As you walk, you become aware of someone walking with you. The rhythm of their footsteps matches yours. Your awareness of this person increases, and you begin to feel a powerful glow of joyful energy move through you. You turn to look and realise that you are accompanied by a young and beautiful child who smiles playfully at you.

The child's eyes glisten with happiness and love as she speaks your name. She reaches out both her hands towards you. Your hands touch and you instantly feel a spark of energy rush through you. You feel your body transform into that of a child. Your companion laughs and begins to playfully pull you towards her. The joy emanating from the child is infectious. She begins to run, and you run excitedly alongside. You spend some time running, skipping, dancing, and laughing together.

You begin to enjoy your freedom of movement and spirit, and you find yourself laughing with joy. After a while, you are both so exhausted that you fall to the ground laughing together. You both turn to lie on your back and watch the clouds move gently overhead. You are aware of the sound of the child's breath next to you. You turn to look at her and she reaches to the ground, picks a flower, and hands it to you. As you take it, you are filled with a glow of absolute love. You both rest here for a while enjoying this state of being.

At this point the child may have something to say to you, and/or you may ask her questions. When you have finished the conversation, give thanks by feeling gratitude in your body. It is now time to freely explore the environment with your companion...
(20 minutes)

When the time is up, you finish what you are doing and begin walking through the meadow back to your starting point. The child walks with you for a while and then gradually fades, as she does, you feel yourself growing back into your adult form. You realise you are walking alone. Slowly the image begins to fade and you find yourself back in your room.

Reflect on your experience and record it in your journal.

7 - Step Into Unity

Adult
30 minutes

Slowly allow any images of your room to fade and you find yourself standing in the same thick green grass. You can feel its lush softness under your bare feet. The grass is warm, as it is mid-day, and the Sun is high in the sky. You can feel the heat of the Sun on your skin. You lift your eyes and look out onto a beautiful meadow. There are small crops of colourful spring flowers dotted around, and you can hear the gentle bubbling of a small stream ahead of you. In the distance you can make out a large Oak tree. Its size suggests that it has been here for many years. You feel compelled to walk towards it.

As you walk, you become aware that someone is walking with you. You can hear breathing and you know that you are not alone. The breath is deep and steady. The footsteps are heavy on the ground. You turn your head and find yourself looking directly into deep loving eyes. The woman beside you is wearing a flowing robe of transparent and luminescent fabric which sparkles in the sunlight. She smiles a deep, contented, and knowledgeable smile. The glow of energy within you develops into one of warmth and centredness.

You hear your name spoken, although there is no movement of her mouth, the communication is telepathic. Inside your head you hear the words "come with me", and she turns to the left. You follow, and, as you walk, the sound of running water becomes louder.

I Am God

You soon arrive at the banks of a stream, and then she turns towards you.

She begins to gently remove your clothes and place them carefully on the ground. You feel calm, comfortable, and safe. You know that she is there to help and heal you. When you are fully naked, she reaches out her hands and you put your hands in hers. She leads you into the stream. You welcome the soft cool caress of the water against your naked skin.

You soon reach the centre of the stream, which is knee deep. Here the woman gently lowers you down until you are sitting in the running water up to your waist. She kneels next to you and begins to pour the water over you. Your happiness and inner calm increases with each touch of her hand. You feel a deepening love for her as she washes you lovingly with the water.

She puts her arm around your shoulders and again gently lowers you. You are now lying under the water. You are able to breathe easily and see clearly. The water is iridescent with a rainbow of colours washing over you. You can see the figure above the water smiling down at you, and you know you are safe. As you lay there, you become aware of the feeling that the water is actually washing through you. With each ripple you feel your inner strength increasing. The water cleanses and strengthens you. You feel content, calm, and centred.

When you are ready the woman knows, and she begins to lift you up out of the water. As you stand, you feel

7 - Step Into Unity

exhilarated and powerful, and you and your companion step out of the water.

At this point the woman may have something to say to you and/or you may ask her questions.

When you have finished the conversation you give thanks. Taking your new discoveries with you, it is now time for you and the woman to explore freely...
(20 minutes)

When the time is up, finish what you are doing and begin walking again with your companion through the meadow. As you walk, you realise that she is disappearing. You find yourself walking alone once again. Slowly the image begins to fade and you find yourself back in your room.

Reflect on your experience and record it in your journal.

Elder
30 minutes

Slowly allow any images of the room around you to fade, and you find yourself standing in the same thick green grass — you can feel its lush softness under your bare feet. The grass is cool as it is early evening and the Sun is low in the sky. You can feel a cool, gentle breeze on your skin.

You lift your eyes and look out onto a beautiful meadow. There are crops of colourful spring flowers dotted around, and you can hear the gentle bubbling of a small stream behind you. In the distance you can make out a large Oak tree. Its size suggests that it has been here for many years. You feel compelled to walk towards it.

You begin to near the tree. Its trunk is solid and its roots are spread out beneath it. As you get nearer, you become aware of an older figure standing in front of it. The woman looks almost as if she is part of the tree itself. She is wearing a dark robe, black but iridescent, like the night sky. Her eyes are filled with the knowledge and wisdom that comes with age. The sense of magickal power and strength that flows from her is immense, and you feel your own magick and power gaining strength as you walk towards her.

She reaches out her hands and you immediately put yours into hers. A huge wave of relief washes through you as you make contact. She knows and understands

7 - Step Into Unity

you completely. She leads you around the vast trunk of the tree into the long evening shadows behind.

There is a large cauldron bubbling and steaming away. Every colour is swirling inside it. You know that this is where her gift for you lies. She wants you to reach in for yourself but you are hesitant at first. You walk slowly towards the cauldron. As you get closer, the sound of the swirling power becomes so loud it fills your whole being.

You raise your arms and then plunge them deeply into the cauldron. The lights and colours swim through you, and, for this moment, you are in contact with everything in the universe, you have access to all knowledge and all wisdom. You feel the lights and colours moving through you, entering every cell, and all the gaps in-between.

Breathe here... experience this moment.

You feel something touching your hands and you wrap your fingers around it. You remove your arms from the cauldron and then hold them high above your head. Looking up you can see the gift in your hands. Energy flows out of you in all directions and you experience the feeling of all power and all love.

At this point, the ancient one may have something to say to you, and/or you may ask her any questions.

When you have finished the conversation you give thanks. Taking your new discoveries with you it is now time to explore freely with your elder...

(20 minutes).

When the time is up, you finish what you are doing and give thanks. The elder directs you back around the tree.

The Sun is now setting below the horizon, and you see the lights and colours that you now hold within you reflected in the beautiful sunset. With the gift still held firmly in your hands you walk away from the tree, back the way that you came. Slowly the image begins to fade, and you find yourself back in your room.

Reflect on your experience and record it in your journal.

The Divine Marriage
1 hour

It is now time to accept and acknowledge your learning so far and to ritually integrate all that you are. This will take the form of a divine marriage ritual where you will make vows to yourself and join all the facets of your being into one. To become whole is to become divine.

To prepare:

- ❖ Before you begin, take some time to reflect on the following and write down your thoughts.

    - I love myself because...
    - I forgive all my past 'mistakes' because...
    - In order to honour my divine self I will...

- ❖ Within the ritual you may wish to use the words you write here, and/or other words that may come to you in the moment.
- ❖ Prepare a gift for yourself. It could be a ring or some other item of jewellery. It could be a picture that reminds you of your divine light.
- ❖ Build your personal Astral Temple. What would you choose as your most beautiful sacred place? It could be a place in nature, underwater, deep in the cosmos, or it could be a beautiful building or a fabric-swathed tent. Close your eyes and imagine this for a while. Build it for yourself in your mind. Give it colour and decoration. In your Astral

Temple you will need a source of fresh water, a bed, and an altar with your sacred objects on it.
❖ You may wish to change some of the words below. Make this ritual your own.

Prepare your space by laying out your gift to yourself, any words that you have written, and your magickal robe. Begin this ritual naked. Follow the instructions in appendix 1.

Slowly allow any images to fade and begin to visualise yourself entering your Astral Temple. There is food laid out for you and people are here to help you prepare. They gently remove your clothes and then wash you with water that sparkles so brightly it might be filled with powdered precious jewels. At the same time, you are being fed with all your favourite foods. Eventually the people dry you and then lay you down on the soft bed. You are given a sensual and intimate massage with deeply perfumed oils.

Take plenty of time to fully enjoy the sensuality of this experience. Move your hands over your physical body to reflect the actions of the people in the Astral Temple. Give yourself permission to move in response to their touch and make sounds if you need to.

When the massage is finished they help you to sit and then stand. You see someone walking towards you carrying fabric of your favourite colour. They hold it up. It is your magickal robe. It seems to be made of the very lightest, almost translucent, cloth. Your arms are held up and the robe is placed over your body. At this

7 - Step Into Unity

point, with care and reverence, put on your physical magickal clothing (if you don't have any, remain naked). Try to hold on to your deep state of meditation while you do this.

The people begin to move you towards your altar. When you arrive, you see the Spirits of the four Elements standing around you. On the altar is a box with the word 'name' engraved on it. You know that inside is the name that reflects your deepest and truest nature. You carefully open the box and find your magickal name, either in written or symbolic form.

With your eyes closed you now stand up in your own physical sacred space and, holding your arms out in front of you with your palms facing upwards, you say:

"Great Divine Spirit within and without me, that is 'I' in connection with my divine. Enter into me so that I may accept my Truth with love."

Hold your head back slightly and raise your sternum. With a smile, and on an inhale, feel yourself being filled with divine light. Breathe with this experience for a while then bring your head forward again and say:

"Today I will give myself [speak everyday name] to myself [speak new magickal name].

I love myself because... [speak the words you have already written and/or intuit words in the moment].

I forgive all my past mistakes because... [speak the words you have already written and/or intuit words in the moment].

In order to honour my divine self I will... [speak the words you have already written and/or intuit words in the moment].

Say:

"I am devoted to the journey of self-realisation and to the manifestation of my divine presence into the physical world.

Above me I am the stars and below me I am the Earth.

Like the stars I am a constant source of unique sparkling light.

Like the Earth I am a firm foundation from which my divine being can grow.

My divine light will manifest in this body.

With all that I am and all that I have, I honour ME.

I take ME as my partner and my eternal love.

I will walk my true path from this day and forever.

I am that I am"

Now present yourself with the gift you have prepared and say:

"May this gift inspire me to passionately follow my true path. I wear/keep it with honour knowing it represents the vows I have made to my divine self."

Sit down and meditate on your experience. Follow the instructions in appendix 2.

Divine Union – Sacred Sex Magick
Usually around 1 – 2 hours.

During the next week or so, having made the marriage, it will be time to consummate. This practice will allow you to experience the blissful state of union and to concretise the sacred marriage. When we experience this in a magickal state it is then much more possible to bring the knowledge into everyday life and eventually to experience union in every moment. It is no coincidence that monotheist state religions are obsessed with sex. They know of the immense power of the sacred sexual act and they want to keep this knowledge to themselves. As I described in the very beginning of this book, the story of the Garden of Eden warns you vehemently to abstain from sex (knowledge). However, it's now time to bite, suck, lick, and swallow the apple.

Take this ritual slowly and do not pressure yourself in any way. Hold no expectations and simply allow it to be what it is. It will offer you a different experience every time you do it.

> *Follow the instructions in appendix 1 to prepare.*
>
> *Lie down with your knees bent, your feet on the floor, your legs slightly apart, and your arms wide, or sit cross-legged.*
>
> *Focus on your breath. Imagine that when you inhale you are taking in light-filled energy from the environment around you. Visualize this energy as shining golden or luminescent particles. See/feel them*

entering your body from all directions and giving you strength, energy, and inspiration. As you exhale, imagine that you are releasing anything left that is blocking you from your sacred path to self-realisation. Exhale anything that is blocking you from embracing your divinity. Enjoy the sensations of receiving and releasing breath and energy for a while.

Now, as you inhale, suck the air through your lips as if you were breathing though a wide straw, making a gentle sucking sound. Begin to take deeper and longer breaths expanding into your belly. Relax your pelvis backwards and gently arch your spine to create more space for the breath as you expand your abdomen.

Continue to take in the light-energy and feel it entering your body also through your genital area. Draw it up into your body and up through your spine with the breath, all the way up through the top of your head.

At the same time, use one or both of your hands to reflect the journey of light and power by tracing your fingers from your genital area to your forehead with each inhale. Visualise your physical and astral body illuminating, inch by inch, as the light, your hand, and your breath travel upwards.

As you exhale relax your lips and jaw and allow a gentle 'aaahhh' sound. Using your pelvic-floor muscles, draw your pelvis forward, and round your back slightly. Have the sense of pushing the energy out of the top of your head. Visualize the energy pouring out like a light-filled rainbow fountain. Watch as it flows back

7 - Step Into Unity

down and around your body, ready to enter you again from below. At the end of the exhale gently place your hands back on your genital area.

Imagine that you are circulating and integrating everything about the universe and yourself – all that you are, all that you have been, and all that you will be. Raise the corners of your mouth into a smile and feel immense love for your past, present, and future divine self. Recognise your physical body as a manifestation of your divine consciousness.

Allow this to continue as long as you want. As you open to this channel of light entering and moving through your body, your passion may be ignited. Let the practice be as intimate/sexual as you feel ready for. Allow your fingers to awaken your body's sensations as they travel up and down. If it feels right, touch your genitals with one hand to awaken your sexual energy even more, while your other hand continues the journey up and down. This reconnects your heart with your sex and your manifest being with your spirit.

As you become increasingly sexually aroused you may find yourself wanting to hold your breath and remain still and quiet. But do not. If you keep the breath rhythm flowing it will create a far more profound experience. Don't let the mind wander away from the circular breath and visualisation – a few seconds of faster panting of the breath before going back to the rhythmical breathing can bring the focus back again. Allow this to continue for as long as you wish. Take your time to build the sexual energy. As you begin to feel the first waves of orgasm, or when you feel that the energy is reaching a powerful point, keep the sound, breath, and body moving and, speed up the rhythm of your breath.

As you reach your peak of energy take 30 or so very quick panting breaths.

Then do the following:

- ❖ *Take three deep breaths*
- ❖ *On the third inhale, hold your breath.*
- ❖ *Bring your attention to the area just above the top of your head, from where the fountain of light springs.*
- ❖ *Raise your eyes up inside your head as if looking above you.*
- ❖ *Press your tongue against the soft palette in the roof of your mouth.*
- ❖ *Tense every muscle in your body.*
- ❖ *Visualise yourself as the divine being that you are.*

All of the above will draw the sexual energy up and around your body. This allows the whole energetic and physical body to experience the light-filled ecstasy of this moment, while energising and integrating the belief in yourself as a divine being.

When you can no longer hold the breath...

Exhale...

7 - Step Into Unity

Allow your body to express any movements and sounds that arise naturally. You may find your body shaking or convulsing; you may experience tears; you may experience yourself as the blissful eternal sea of collective and universal consciousness. Whatever happens, breathe freely and ride this wave of ecstatic experience.

When your body becomes still, rest for a while.

After some time, when you feel ready, carefully stand up with a wide stance, your arms stretched outward, your sternum slightly raised, and your head up.

Repeat the following, continuously until it becomes a rhythmical chant:

*"I am that I am,
I am that I am,
I am that I am..."*

Continue to repeat the chant, but allow it to become quieter and quieter, until it becomes a whisper... then a silent voice... then a chant in your mind...

Begin to feel the rhythm of the chant reflecting in your body. If you later connect with it in your everyday life it will instantly remind you of this experience. Chant it to refrain from 'little-you' re-actions. Chant it as a way to be totally present and in love. Chant it to remind yourself that you are wholly responsible for your creations.

Finally sit down and feel. Be in this moment and witness the changes in your body.

When you are ready to finish, follow the instructions in appendix 2.

This ritual can also be used for <u>any kind of magickal creation work</u>. Simply replace the intention, the chant, and the visualisation with whatever you would like to create. However it is one of the most powerful forms of magick and should be used only with full integrity. Think long and hard about what you want to create because it *will* manifest.

Be careful what you wish for!

7 - Step Into Unity

Know Everything Be Everywhere

Having unified with your inner divine being, and experienced the blissful union with All, you will have wisdom enough to open to the experience of truths and vibrations far beyond your previous understanding. Following are a few practices that will enable you to discover all knowledge and to move beyond any everyday problems.

Cellular and Energetic Healing
30 minutes or more

When you are in connection with the divine, and feel you can really trust your inner wisdom, it is possible to ask your unconscious to heal itself.

> *Follow the instructions in appendix 1 to prepare.*
>
> *When you are ready, take a visual journey into your body, to the source of pain/discomfort. Look around, explore, and magnify the area. Look at the bones, the organs, and deep into the cells. What is going on? Can you see anything unusual? Are there any dark patches or cold areas? What are the colours?*
>
> *Ask your body what it needs.*
>
> ❖ *Sometimes the healing can be as simple as bringing light into the area.*

- *Sometimes you may need to manipulate or massage bones, muscles, sinews, or organs, either as part of your visualisation or physically.*
- *You may need to encourage your immune system to clear the area, using visualisations and communications.*
- *You may be given information about particular herbs, treatments, or activities that will help.*
- *You may need to lie down and allow the body to heal. Just drop deeply into your body and circulate energy around your cellular structure. This can cause shaking and spasming. Trust that your body knows what it needs, and allow these (sometimes very strange) sounds and movements to occur.*

When you have finished follow the instructions in appendix 2

This method can be used to help other people too. In an awakened and aware state you will be able to see things by 'looking into their physical body', or by sensing their auric field with your hands. You will be able to bring healing by drawing light/love to the person, or to the specific area (bearing in mind that we are whole beings and areas of ill-health affect the whole body/psyche). Just having the intention to heal, and moving your hands through someone's energetic field, is often enough, if you are fully in tune with your divine self.

However beware. Only work in this way if you are 100% certain that you are not being led by ego and a need to be appreciated, liked, or adored for your 'amazing' skills. NEVER do it without the permission and request of the person involved. It is not your responsibility to choose when someone should be healed.

I have met many healers who have taken great delight in establishing some kind of power over vulnerable people by showing off their knowledge and attempting to prove that they know the person they are working with better than the person knows themself. If you do work with another person remember that everything you see is symbolic and should never be described literally.

For example I once heard a 'healer' saying the following frightening statement: "I can see your spine crumbling"! Anything you say to someone can set up a belief structure in them and they will eventually manifest it as their reality. So be careful. Ask questions rather than making statements. For example: 'How does it feel here?' or 'What do you notice here?' Remember you have nothing to prove. The trust that people place in you must be absolutely respected at all times and you should treat them with love and great care. Only work with other people when you are in a clear and awakened state. It is an enormous responsibility and can change people's lives.

Heal Traumatic Memories
30 minutes or more

As I have said, it may be that your emotional/physical pain or illness is due to a traumatic experience in the past that has been held in your body. Trauma creates deep pathways in the mind leaving us with memories and stories from which our behaviour, beliefs, emotions, and actions are then driven.

For example, the trauma of a violent parent may lead you to believe a story that you are unlovable and/or always in danger. You will live your life as if this story was true and you will see 'evidence' of it everywhere. This will affect you in many ways. For example, you may not believe it when someone tells you 'I love you', and you may find it difficult to trust people, which could cause relationships to break down.

Whatever your stories are, it is unhelpful to continue to believe them. But it's not possible to simply disbelieve them. You may need to go back to the memories and heal them from the source. The practice below offers another method for you to rewrite the stories that were created during moments or periods of trauma. You may need to repeat it a few times if the particular memory you are working on is very ingrained.

Follow the instructions in appendix 1.

❖ *Visualise the memory as a scene. In the first instance, remember it exactly as it happened, but see the scene in black and white rather than in*

7 - Step Into Unity

colour. *Try not to engage with the emotions of the scene just watch it as if from a distance.*

❖ *When the scene has finished, allow it to lose all its clarity and watch as it dissipates, dissolves, shrinks, or flies away.*

❖ *Exhale and feel a sense of letting it go. Stand up and shake or wriggle your body to release any associated physical/emotional tension or stress that arose during the visualisation.*

❖ *Next, when you feel ready, re-live the scene in a different way, this time changing it into a story of little-you being loved and cared for, rather than hurt.*

❖ *See the new scene in full sparkling colour and allow yourself to feel the full emotion of the safety and love. Smile and inhale the happy feelings into your body.*

❖ *Sometimes people find it difficult to imagine parents changing to a different way of being, so bringing an angel, an Elemental spirit, a new 'good parent', or even your own adult divine-self, into the scene may be more helpful.*

❖ *Watch as the safe and loving 'being' steps into the scene and gives you exactly what you need. It may be just that they hold you and love you, it may be that they take you away from the scene, or it may be that they help you to feel strong and empowered enough to say 'no!' to whoever was hurting you. Feel the safety and love.*

Finish with the Angel Love meditation on page 116. Reflect on your experience then follow the instructions in appendix 2.

Inter-dimensional Travel
30 minutes

This journey can be used to step into the experience of another 'life', another being, another thing, or another reality. You may also experience what feels like a journey into the past or the future (as you may have already noticed from the previous practices time is not a relevant dimension when working on this level). This practice can be used to learn a new skill, find out information, or to simply discover new experiences and therefore widen your wisdom, understanding, and vision. The experiences this ritual can evoke are common for people on a mystical path. They are very powerful and often feel very real. People/religions/mystics have explained them in the following different ways:

- ❖ Past/future lives – you are entering a life you have lived before or will live in the future.
- ❖ Akashic Records – everything and every experience is recorded in a universal astral library or database, and it is this that you are exploring.
- ❖ Quantum Leaping – all time (including parallel life) is happening simultaneously, and it is possible to leap into your own 'other life' or into someone or something else's life (past, present, or future).
- ❖ Shapeshifting – entering the body of an animal (or other thing) or having it enter you.

The names you choose to identify your experience are not really relevant to the process. I prefer to simply be with my experience rather than to get bogged down with meaning

7 - Step Into Unity

and intellectual debate. It is unnecessary and can even limit the experience by fixing its meaning to just one thing.

Before you start the practice you could decide to explore something specific. For example you might want to:

- ❖ Understand what it feels like to be a particular animal.
- ❖ Experience an event of interest – e.g. a death, a birth, a time in history, or the future.
- ❖ Enter the experience of an historical figure – e.g. an Egyptian pharaoh or a mediaeval queen.
- ❖ Understand the experience of another thing – a rock, the earth, or a tree.
- ❖ Explore life on other planets or in other galaxies.
- ❖ Learn a new skill by entering the experience of a craftsperson, an expert, or someone who speaks another language.

Either set an intention before you start or decide to be open to any experience your consciousness directs you towards.

Follow the instructions in appendix 1 to prepare.

Begin to visualise a vortex of rainbow light spinning around you. Sense the air in the room moving. As you start to believe that you are inside this powerful whirlpool of energy, you begin to experience the sensation of being lifted out of your body. Feel yourself circling and being pulled deeper and deeper into it. Experience the sensation of travelling at great speed through time and space, and feel yourself rising higher and higher. Make the experience real and powerful in your mind.

When the time is right, you feel everything stop very suddenly. You can feel yourself spinning and falling. Eventually you have a very clear experience of 'landing'. First, notice yourself – what/who are you, what do you look like, and what do you feel like? Then widen your focus, notice the environment, the landscape, the sense of time, and other beings or people.

Explore and learn... (20 minutes)

When you have finished, take care to make the journey back to your current and everyday experience. Go back to your starting point. Visualise the same vortex of rainbow light spinning around you. Make this image strong, and sense the air moving around you as well. Experience yourself being lifted out of the body (or thing) that you were inhabiting and then entering the whirlpool. Feel the sensation of travelling at great speed through time and space, higher and higher. When the time is right, you feel everything stop very suddenly, then you begin to fall, and you eventually have a very clear experience of 'landing' in your physical space of this here and now.

When you have finished, sit with your experience for a while and record it in your journal.

Then follow the instructions in appendix 2.

Speak Your Divine Truth
40 minutes

This ritual will allow you to contact your inner knowledge and then speak it out-loud. Like a priestess, a priest, a guru, a teacher, or a divine being, universal wisdom will flow out of you. This ritual often brings the most profound insights. You may want to record it.

Follow the instructions in appendix 1 to prepare, and then, to raise the energy, repeat the **divine union ritual** *(p.279) to the point just before the orgasmic or energetic peak.*

Stand up with your sternum raised and your palms upwards. Repeat:

"I am, I am, I am, I am..." find a rhythm with this. Allow your body to follow it with movement. Continue this chant and movement for 5-10 minutes.

Next, continue to speak the words out-loud and, this time, allow your divine wisdom to finish your sentences:

"I am...
I am...
I am..."

Allow the words to come without preparation or thought. Continue until you feel you have exhausted the words...

Then continue more, until again you feel as though you have finished...

Then continue more, digging deeper, stretching further...

Keep going for 5-10 minutes more.

When you have spoken from your deepest wisdom using 'I am...' continue further, but now say anything your divine wisdom needs to speak of...

Allow the words to come...
No self-judgement or criticism...
Allow yourself to speak the words of truth...

When it feels like you've finished, wait, breathe deeper into the silence... no thinking...

Speak more...

Again, when it feels like you've finished, wait, dig deeper, stretch further, and speak more.

Allow at least 10 minutes, but keep going for as long as you need.

When you have finished speaking from your divine wisdom, sit in silence for a while. Reflect on the things you heard yourself say. Breathe with the universe.

Follow the instructions in appendix 2.

7 - Step Into Unity

Know Unity

This meditation will join you with the infinite universal vibration. In the process of this practice you will come to know all of time and all of existence. You will know its simplicity and you will know its magnitude. However, to know true Unity, you must first understand polarity.

In magick, mysticism, spirituality, and religion there is much reference to the 'female' and the 'male' or the 'feminine' and the 'masculine' 'polarity'. In religious belief systems, this is often personified as goddess and god. This relates to, and encourages, the belief that sexual gender in living things reflects a clear binary opposition. It also offers this supposed difference in a misleading and usually misogynist, way. This idea of 'gender' is often also misinterpreted in magickal circles, when practitioners mistake the symbols of 'female' and 'male' as somehow relating to sexual gender or to woman and man.

However in mystical practice and magick the correct interpretation of the terms 'male and female' have NOTHING to do with actual men or women, or sexual gender in anything. These words refer to <u>energy flow only</u>! In magick and/or religion there is a danger (or a useful tool in the wrong hands) in misinterpreting 'energetic gender' as 'sexual gender'. It has led to gender based discrimination and hierarchical systems within cultures. The problematic misunderstanding, and the common faulty associations of the symbolism of polarised gender, is as follows:

POSITIVE	NEGATIVE
ACTIVE	PASSIVE
LIGHT	DARK
WHITE	BLACK
GOOD	BAD
GOD	DEVIL – monotheist
GOD	GODDESS – polytheist
MALE	FEMALE

However, when you remove the idea of sexual gender (which is not a binary opposite anyway), and the religious ideas of 'good versus bad', that arose due to the misunderstanding of the meaning of energetic polarity, the meaning of this universal force of nature becomes clear.

The POSITIVE AND NEGATIVE polarity relates to electromagnetic forces, or magnetic poles, and other events in natural phenomena where there is an opposing but balancing force, for example:

POSITIVE	NEGATIVE
REPELLING	DRAWING-IN
FULL	EMPTY
GIVE	RECIEVE/TAKE
ON	OFF
LIGHT	DARK

When understood properly this idea of 'energetic gender' can act as a stepping stone towards experiencing the true nature of first duality and eventually unity.

Unity Breath Meditation
40 minutes

Follow the instructions in appendix 1 to prepare.

PART 1 – POLARITY

When your mind is clear of thoughts, bring your awareness back to your breath. Focus simply on the inhale and the exhale. Be gentle with the breath, simply notice. Find your natural rhythm of in... and out...

As you inhale, feel yourself opening to fresh energy.

As you exhale, feel yourself releasing the breath.

As you inhale, expand and visualise yourself lighting up and switching on.

As you exhale, contract and visualise yourself darkening and switching off.

As you inhale feel yourself coming alive. Notice how the breath rushes in to fill the vacuum of the emptiness.

As you exhale feel yourself releasing again to death.

In this simple action you are one with everything in the universe. Everything gives and receives, everything expands and contracts, and everything is on and off.

I Am God

As you breathe – in and out – have a sense of your connection to this moment and to the rhythms of the universe, feel yourself at one with All.

Sit with this knowledge of yourself as a part of this great whole. Feel it...

Breathe in…. breathe out ...

Feel...

There is nothing except in and out...

Contraction and expansion...
Giving and receiving...
On and off...

Notice the difference between the two opposing forces...
Notice the beauty of each...
Notice the quality of each
Notice the necessity for each...

This is all there is...

There is nothing else in the universe except this moment, this breath, and this rhythm.

Repeat silently:
At the peak of the inhale – "I am every-thing"
At the peak of the exhale – "I am no-thing"

Sit with this polarity for at least 5 minutes.

7 - Step Into Unity

PART 2 – JOIN OPPOSING FORCES

Now let these thoughts go and begin to focus on the gap between the inhales and the exhales. Begin to gently hold your breath in order to extend this gap. Don't hold it to the point of pain, but remain calm and relaxed and let the breath go just before this (with practice this gap in the breath will become longer).

Inhale. Gently hold the breath and, just before you exhale, experience this moment of 'alive'...

Before you release again to 'death'...

Exhale then gently hold the breath, and, just before you inhale, feel this moment of 'death'...

Before you reclaim 'life'...

Focus on these gaps for 5 minutes.

Now, breathing normally, bring the breath and the gaps together, begin to experience them as a constant flow.

As your emptiness fills up with the inhale focus on the upcoming exhale.

As the breath is released with the exhale, sense the next inhale ready and waiting to come in.

Sit with this circular and endless nature of the breath for 5 minutes. Give and receive simultaneously.

PART 3 – EXPERIENCE UNITY

Let go of the focus on breath...
Let go of the focus on the gaps...

Simply cease to notice.

Be only in the moment – this moment of infinite Unity. There is no separation, no self, no identity, and no definition. Stay here...

The experience of Unity may come for only a second during this practice, or more, or less. Don't look for it. It will come when you are ready. If it comes and then goes again, don't chase it. It might come again, it might not.

However, no matter how often you feel it, or for how long, it will be blissful and ecstatic. If you are truly experiencing it, time will not be an issue, as it will be a boundless and infinite moment.

To know Unity even for one second is to know that you are divine. This will change your life forever.

Breathe gently and radiate blissful love in all directions. Take time to reflect and then follow the instructions in appendix 2.

*

In Unity you are All, One, everything, everywhere, and you are infinite. In Unity you are divine.

*

Here's where I'll Leave You to Explore…

Through the practice in this book you have travelled from the inner world to the outer cosmos and beyond – into the infinite Unity, that is YOU in your divine presence. These journeys and rituals will always bring you new insights and new growth, no matter how often you use them. I have practiced all of these journeys and rituals hundreds of times over the years, and each time I am astounded at the wisdom I find there. Your internal wisdom and the collective consciousness are endless sources of information, knowledge, learning, and healing.

I hope you have enjoyed working through the practices and experiences. Now you have all the tools you need in order to step freely into life and into your full power. Keep up the work and you will continue to grow into yourself.

You will be amazed at who you can become.

Continuing the **foundation breath meditation,** the **body sensation meditation,** the **thought awareness meditation,** or the **unity breath meditation** on a daily basis will help you to sustain your growth and your learnings. Your mind may attempt to 'talk' you out of your daily practice, but if you work to keep it up you will benefit greatly. By simply watching your thought processes and your sensations, without reacting, you will remind yourself to avoid the drama of running towards pleasure and away from pain. You will remain calm and balanced, you will be fully able to enjoy the experience of NOW, and you will have as much passion and freedom of expression as you wish.

Trust your insights and your intuition. They will lead you onto your true path. Try not to be swayed by the influence of other people, remember, they may still be living in a world of fear. Take the risks that you need to take, and leap into your wildness with love.

When you love and value yourself with no judgements, no expectations, and no conditions, it is so much simpler to love and value others in the same way. This will bring endless joy and happiness to you, and to the people around you.

You have the right to channel your own personal genius, whatever this is. You are unique – no one else can offer what you can offer.

You are perfect in all that you are.

Shine your light and bring the gift of YOU into the world.

The world will be a much better place for it.

Lilith Speaks

God,

I see you.

Can you see yourself?

You are HERE, and you are NOW – a beautiful manifestation of divinity. I love you… I love All that you are.

Within you I can see the reflection of all aspects of the great divine wisdom. I can see in you all vibration and all connection. You are love, you are ecstasy, you are infinite light, you are being, you are bliss, and you are Truth.

You are the divine manifest.
You are All of nature and the universe.

Go out into the wild and commune with all that you are. Roar your song into the furthest reaches of the universe. Love with shameless passion and speak your powerful words of creation. Dance your story and embrace All.

Fear no more… you are free.

I bow to you with absolute reverence.

I love you because I am you.

I am God…

and so are you.

Appendix 1 – Before All Magickal Work

The Ritual of the Sacred Circle
Foundation Breath Meditation
To Begin

The Ritual of the Sacred Circle

Call the Spirit of Air

- Face the East.
- Light the yellow candle, or your single white candle, and hold it up.
- Inhale the energy of the Element Air.
- Hold awareness of your intellect and your mind, and smile to lighten your thoughts.
- Visualise your Air thought-form facing you and say:

"Spirit of Air,
bringing life and light from the East.
You who offer clarity of mind,
focused thought,
and open the doors to clear communication.
The eagle, the hummingbird, and the fairies.
The wide open skies, the soft clouds,
and the air I breathe.
Be here this day.
Let darkness and light reside in balance and harmony.
Welcome Spirit of Air"

- Draw the Air pentagram with your candle.
- Walk around the room clockwise drawing a large circle with the candle. Imagine that you are drawing the energy of Air around you.
- Put down the candle at the Air altar and pick up your chosen Air object. Hold it with intent, facing the East, and say:

"Let this… (put the name of your object here – 'cup', 'chalice' etc.)… be filled with the power of Air"

- Place it down again.

Call the Spirit of Fire

- If you have just one candle, carry it to the Fire altar. If you have a different candle in each quarter, take the Fire candle and light it from the Air candle.
- Turn to face the South.
- Hold up the candle.
- Inhale the energy of Fire.
- Feel your passion and creative flow and smile to bring sparkles to your body.
- Visualise your thought-form for Fire facing you and say:

*"Spirit of Fire,
bringing warmth and health from the South.
You who offer passion, creative energy,
and open the doors to intuition.
The salamander, the phoenix,*

and the dragon.
The heat of the sun, the warmth of the hearth, and the pleasure in my belly.
Be here this day.
Let darkness and light reside in balance and harmony.
Welcome Spirit of Fire"

- Draw the Fire pentagram with your candle.
- Walk around the room clockwise, drawing a circle with the candle. Imagine that you are drawing the power of Fire around you.
- Put down the candle at the Fire altar and pick up your chosen Fire object. Hold it with intent, still facing the South, and say:

"Let this... (name your object)... be filled with the power of Fire"

- Place your object down again.

Call the Spirit of Water

- If you have just one candle, carry it to the Water altar. If you have a different candle in each quarter, take the Water candle and light it from the Fire candle.
- Face the West.
- Hold up the candle.

- Inhale the energy of Water.
- Feel your emotion and flow, and smile to bring softness to your heart.
- Visualise your Water thought-form facing you and say:

"Spirit of Water,
bringing love and union from the West.
You who offer emotional flow,
psychic vision,
and open the doors to deep connection.
The dolphins, the mermaids,
and the water nymphs.
The tidal shifts, the ripples on the lakes, and the deep love
in my heart.
Be here this day.
Let darkness and light reside in balance and harmony.
Welcome spirit of Water"

- Draw the Water pentagram with your candle.
- Walk around the room clockwise, drawing a circle with your candle. Imagine that you are drawing the energy of Water around the circle.
- Put the candle down at the Water altar and pick up your Water object. Hold it with intent towards the west.

"Let this... (name your object)... be filled with the power of Water"

- Place your object down again.

Call the Spirit of Earth

- If you have a single candle, carry it to the Earth altar. If you have a different candle in each quarter, take the Earth candle and light it from the Water candle.
- Face the North.
- Hold up the candle.
- Breathe in the energy of Earth.
- Feel your feet firmly grounded and connected with the planet Earth.
- Visualise your thought-form for the Element of Earth facing you and say:

"Great Spirit of Earth,
Bringer of the mountains and the trees from the North.
You who offer my food, my home,
and open the doors to the manifest world.
The four footed beasts, the goat,
and the centaur.
The earth beneath me, the life around me,
and my own sensual body.
Be here this day.
Let darkness and light reside in balance and harmony.
Welcome spirits of Earth"

- Draw the Earth pentagram with your candle.
- Walk around the room clockwise, drawing a circle with the candle. Imagine that you are drawing the energy of Earth around the circle.
- Put down the candle and pick up your Earth object. Hold it with intent towards the North and say:

"Let this... (name your object)... be filled with the power of Earth"

- Place your object down again.
- If you have just one candle, walk back to the Eastern quarter and place it there to complete the circle.
- If you have four candles, walk to the Eastern candle and touch the two flames together to complete the circle. Then place the green candle back on the Earth altar.

Call the Centre

- Visualise the circle of shimmering white light around you.
- Visualise the pentagrams where you drew them in the air with the candle flames and your thought-form Spirits of Earth, Water, Fire, and Air standing (or floating) in their directions.
- Visualise two triangles, one with its base on the ground pointing upwards the other high above you pointing downwards.
- Visualise them moving towards each other in a straight line until they meet at a point just above the centre of the circle creating a six-pointed star.

- Roll your eyes up inside your head and watch as it glows with golden light. Contemplate the manifest and the non-manifest becoming one.
- Visualise a great pyramid surrounding you – the star at its apex.
- As you stand inside the pyramid feel your feet at its base
- Visualise your roots stretching deep into the planet Earth. Then raise your arms above your head, pointing to the top of the pyramid.
- Visualise your fingers growing into roots which reach up into the sky, out into the solar system, further out into the greater cosmos, and then deep into the infinite universes.
- Feel yourself opening to all possibilities, imagine yourself in a gap of silence, between words, between thought, and open yourself to cosmic consciousness.

Say:

> *"In the centre of the great pyramid,*
> *below me the Earth and above me the sky.*
> *Around me the flaming pentagrams and the circle of light.*
> *Above me the six-rayed star.*
> *This place is sealed."*

Call the Higher Power – Spirit

Raise your arms up, breathe deeply, and say:

> *"Divine Spirit within and without.*
> *I – all of nature and the universe.*

I – all Power. I – all creation. I – all Love.
Lead me to wisdom and understanding.
Lead me to do my work and realise my full potential
– to live and serve my divine truth.
Welcome Divine Spirit"

Sit down in your space, breathe, and hold awareness of your personal divinity.

Foundation Breath Meditation

Sit in a relaxed but upright posture, either in a chair or on the floor. Try to keep your spine straight (not tense) in order to work allow the energy in your body to move freely and to stop yourself falling asleep.

Close your eyes and begin to focus on your breath.
As you exhale, allow yourself to release.
Exhale... Release physical tension.
Exhale... Release judgement and analysis.
Exhale... Release all thought.

Continue breathing... watch each breath... notice how it feels to bring air into your body, to feel your lungs and chest expand. Breathe... notice the emptying as you exhale.

Allow your lungs to empty completely... and slowly inhale to your full capacity. Gently exhale completely. Do this 3 times.

Continue to breathe... find your natural rhythm. Let it be, don't try to change it. Ignore thoughts about 'good' breathing or 'bad' breathing, just accept what is.

As you exhale, let go of these or any other thoughts... breathe away self-judgement and criticism... Release physical tension... Release all thought...

Now, as you inhale, allow your expanding breath to energise you, let the breath fill you with swirling energy.... watch your internal world as each inhale brings replenishing nourishment into your body. Do this 3 times.

If a thought comes in… breathe it away on your next exhale… and bring your focus back to the breath….

Breathe… breathe…

Watch… notice every breath…
Do you have any thoughts or judgements… simply notice them… then let them go on the next exhale… breathe them away…. breathe…

Allow the inhale to expand your mind… feel the sense of space there…

Breathe… breathe… breathe…
If a thought comes in, let it go.
Breathe… allow the inhale to expand your consciousness…

Breathe… allow the breath to create space.

Another thought? Catch it… observe it …breathe it out… let it go… then bring your awareness back to the breath.

Breathe… breathe… breathe…

To Begin Every Journey

With your eyes closed, begin to visualise yourself in the room that is around you. See the candles and your altars. Now widen your awareness to include the astral space and visualise the circle of light surrounding you, the pentagrams in the four directions, your thought-form for each of the Spirits of Earth, Water, Fire, and Air. Visualise the pyramid surrounding you and the six-pointed star above you — at the apex of the pyramid. As you roll your eyes up inside your head to look at the six-pointed star you can feel your connection to Divine Spirit. Feel your physical body strong and grounded. As you breathe deeper, become aware of your astral body. Feel its vibration as lighter and freer than your physical body.

Now let go of the image of the physical objects around you and focus only on the astral shapes and the thought-forms. Next, leaving your physical body where it is, allow your astral body to stand up in your sacred circle and visualise all the sacred shapes surrounding you. Slowly allow all this to fade. Then follow the instructions for the journeys.

Appendix 2 – After All Magickal Work

To End Every Journey

When the images of the journey fade, you find yourself standing once again in your room. Let the images of the astral shapes fade also and begin to notice again the material objects in your room. You can see your physical body sitting in the space. As you watch, your physical body breathes, and you feel drawn towards it.

With each breath you feel more and more connected and you allow yourself to fully re-enter your physical body. As you breathe, you begin to feel the breath moving your body and you can feel the weight of your body against the floor or the chair. When you are ready, take three deep, energising and awakening breaths and open your eyes.

Release the Circle

Face the centre and say:

> "Great divine spirit within and without.
> I thank you for being here with me this day.
> I thank you for offering me the wisdom and the understanding to do my work,
> To know, in order to serve truth.
> Until I call again,
> Hail and farewell"

Visualise your divine spirit, and then watch as it, and the sacred shapes, dissipate into the vibrational surroundings.

Extinguish the candles, starting with the Air candle and moving around the circle clockwise. As you do this visualise your spirit of each Element bowing to acknowledge their departure and feel a strong sense of gratitude. Then say:

"Open may this circle be"

Appendix 3 – Condensed Ritual of the Sacred Circle

When you feel that you have repeated the ritual of the sacred circle enough times so that your consciousness has become fully aligned with the intention of the practice. It is possible to use a shortened version. Although the full ritual is a wonderful practice and if you have the time and inclination it is worth continuing to use it (I have used it weekly for over 25 years). However, if you are short of time, or in a smaller space, or if you don't have your candles/sacred objects, then the ritual below can be used instead.

Stand with your arms open, your sternum raised and your head held slightly back. Experience yourself as the centre point of the universe. Facing the East, visualise the thought forms of Earth, Water, Fire, and Air around you, take three long breaths and say:

> *"Before me Spirit of Air – honest communication and clarity of mind,*
> *To my right side, Spirit of Fire – passion, intuition, and creative expression,*
> *Behind me, Spirit of Water – emotional flow and psychic vision,*
> *To my left side, Spirit of Earth – body, home, and the manifest world."*

Visualise the circle of white light and the flaming pentagrams. Visualise the pyramid and the six-rayed star glowing with golden light. Visualise yourself as a being of eternal light.

Say:

> *"I am Divine Spirit within and without*
> *'I' am all of nature and the universe*
> *'I' all power*
> *'I' all mighty*
> *'I' all love*
> *I am wisdom and understanding*
> *I live and serve my divine truth"*

Sit down in your space, breathe, and feel into your divine power.

Now you can start your magickal working.

To release the circle:

At the end of your work visualise the images of the sacred shapes dissipating into the energetic field around you. Bow gently, with gratitude, to the Spirits of Earth, Water, Fire, and Air knowing that this power is always within you, and use your breath and movement to bring your awareness back to your physical body.

Say: Open may this circle be.

Further Information

Lilith is a teacher, sexual healer, and psychotherapist. If you are inspired by this book and you wish to explore further, either through Lilith's courses, via one-to-one healing, or sacred psychotherapy then please see the website:

www.lilithrising.co.uk